Gary Wilmot, impressionist and comedian, has taken some time off to give you some advice and to help you follow in his footsteps!

From how to mimic your teacher's accent to impersonating Ethel from *EastEnders*, this fun-packed guide tells you all you need to know. Tips on make-up and wigs, sketches to perform and jokes to tell. So, apart from hours of fun and laughs for you and your friends, with Gary's help, you're sure to make THE RIGHT IMPRESSION!

About the author

Gary Wilmot was born in London in May 1954 and has been in show business since 1976. He is a multi-talented entertainer having been seen on television as a comedian, caricaturist–impressionist, singer, dancer, chat-show personality, interviewer and debater. His most recent television series include 'Cue Gary' and 'The Saturday Gang'.

Gary is the Vice-President of the National Boys Clubs. He is married to Carol, a dancer and choreographer, and they have two daughters, Katie and Georgia.

The Right Impression is Gary Wilmot's first book.

GARY WILMOT

WILMOT

THE RIGHT IMPRESSION

GARY WILMOT
AND
MARY DOUGLAS

KNIGHT BOOKS
Hodder and Stoughton

British Library C.I.P.

Wilmot, Gary, *1954–*
   The right impression.
   1. Entertainments.
   Impersonation. Manuals.
   For children
   I. Title   II. Douglas, Mary
   792.7

   ISBN 0-340-42396-X

Printed and bound in Great
Britain for Hodder and Stoughton
Paperbacks, a division of Hodder
and Stoughton Limited, Mill
Road, Dunton Green, Sevenoaks,
Kent TN13 2YA (Editorial Office:
47 Bedford Square, London
WC1B 3DP) by Cox & Wyman Ltd,
Cardiff Road, Reading. Photoset
by Rowland Phototypesetting
Limited, Bury St Edmunds,
Suffolk.

CONTENTS

THE RIGHT IMPRESSION

As far as I can remember, I've always done impressions without really thinking much about them. But I did my first *proper* impression when I was at school. It was of Malcolm Muggeridge, who used to appear in very serious television programmes – the kind that most schoolkids don't watch. I liked him because he had such an expressive voice and an interesting face, but he wasn't really the best choice to start a career as an impressionist with! Whenever I did it half the people would say, 'Isn't it brilliant?' The other half would stand there and say, 'Who's Malcolm Muggeridge?'

That taught me that if you're going to do impressions they'd better be of people the audience can recognise! Most of the impressions that I've outlined in this book are of famous people, like film stars and television personalities, but there's nothing to stop you doing impressions of other, less well-known people. I used to do impressions of my school friends and teachers which used to amuse everyone who knew them. In fact, one of my school reports read: 'Extremely talented if only he would concentrate – but jokes around all the time.' Maybe your milkman has an unusual accent? Or you have an auntie who's always saying silly things? Or a teacher who uses a particular catch-phrase all the time? Why not do an impression of them for your family and friends? If you do it well it could be very funny.

As well as making people laugh, impressions also come in handy when things go wrong. Have you seen me do my Norman Wisdom impression on television? Sometimes in real life when I do something silly, like tripping over or dropping things, I launch into Norman. People are so busy laughing that they forget what happened. Try it out for yourself! Next time you spill something on the living-room carpet go into an instant impression of Peggy from *Hi De Hi* and say, 'Oooh-err, what's Miss Cathcart going to say if she finds out?' With a bit of luck your Mum will laugh so much that she'll forget to be furious with you!

As far as I'm concerned, there's only one rule when it comes to doing impressions: YOU CAN DO AN IMPRESSION OF ANYONE, OR ANY-THING, IN LIFE SO LONG AS YOU DON'T HURT ANYONE'S FEELINGS.

It's really important to remember that im-pressions are intended to make people laugh. If you offend anyone by imitating something that they are very sensitive about, then your im-

pression has failed. Sometimes it can be a difficult thing to judge. For example, my favourite character is Stevie Wonder, who is blind. I really love doing impressions of him, but when I do I have to be very careful not to make fun of his blindness, because that wouldn't be funny. Instead, I concentrate on his songs and voice and the way he moves his head, because they *are* funny. If you suspect that any of your impressions is cruel or would offend anyone, don't do them. *That's the one big rule!*

There's also something else you need to know if you're going to make people laugh, and that's WHEN, AND WHEN NOT, TO DO AN IMPRESSION! There's a time and a place for everything, as the saying goes, and there are some times and some places in which it's best not to do an impression or tell jokes, however funny they may be.

I learned this the hard way – I almost got sacked because I kept messing about and cracking jokes! When I left school, I started training as a carpenter, working under a supervisor. Every few minutes I'd come up with a joke or something silly, and it got to the stage when he said to me, 'I don't want to hear any more jokes! One more and I'm going to the foreman to get you fired.' A few seconds later he said something and I cracked a joke. 'Right,' he said. 'That's it. I've had enough,' and off he went. Fortunately, I didn't get fired, but although the experience didn't stop me joking it made me realise that sometimes you can go too far, even if you're being funny.

Sometimes it's best *not* to show off your impressions. Here are ten crazy examples of occasions when you could find yourself in big trouble if you launch into your favourite comedy impression or don't know when to stop:

1 On a non-stop flight to Australia.
2 During an exam.
3 In a hospital ward full of seriously ill patients. If they laugh, which is unlikely, they might burst their stitches!
4 When someone's dog/cat/budgie has just died or at a funeral.
5 In a police station.
6 When someone is filling out their Income Tax return.
7 During a performance of *Hamlet* at the Royal Shakespeare Theatre – particularly if you are sitting in the front row.
8 When you meet the Queen or any other member of the Royal Family.
9 When you're in a crowded lift and it gets stuck on the twenty-ninth floor.
10 Just as your mother or father is about to reverse into a tiny parking space in a brand new car.

Those are the rules. They're not too bad, are they? Now you know them you can be like me and MAKE THE RIGHT IMPRESSION!

VOICES AND NOISES

When it comes to doing an impersonation, as far as I'm concerned the voice is probably the most important of all the elements I need to get right. Some of my impressions rely almost completely on imitating someone's voice, so if I get that wrong I'm in trouble! I love doing impressions of people with interesting voices but I've found that a lot of them don't work because they don't have a strong enough character or because not many people have heard of them. If you're going to do vocal impressions, choose subjects who have distinctive voices *and* a distinctive character to match.

But before you start doing all those impressions, just think for a minute of all the dozens – hundreds even – of people you can recognise by the sound of their voices alone. The human ear can pick up lots of different voice signals and distinguish between them so that you can even identify people who sound pretty much the same. If you doubt this, why not conduct an experiment?

You'll need a small tape recorder and a short poem or passage from a book. Ask one of your friends to record some volunteers from your class at school reading the poem or passage into the microphone. Don't allow people to say just

what pleases them – insist that they read the text you've chosen. This prevents people giving you clues in the things they say: for example, if your friend Gavin always talks about his gerbils, you'll be able to recognise him from what he says, rather than from the sound of his voice. How many of your classmates' voices can you recognise when the tape is played back? Most of them probably! Now try copying the way some of them speak. It's good practise for your impressions of famous people.

Most people can do easy impressions automatically without bothering to think about technical things like pitch and inflexion that go to make up every voice. They just listen and copy what they hear – that's how I learned to do most of my impressions! But I'm sure you've heard people trying to do impressions and getting it a bit wrong. If you're having trouble getting a voice just right try these tips:

Analysing a voice

If you're finding someone's voice difficult to imitate, try recording it on tape so that you can keep repeating it and playing it back. Listen for the four vital elements that go to make up the way someone sounds – *Pitch*, *Volume*, *Accent* and *Inflexion*.

Pitch describes how high or low the voice is. A man's voice is usually low-pitched, while a woman's is higher-pitched.

Volume describes the loudness or softness of a voice.

Accent is the local or regional way of pronouncing certain words. Most of us can recognise the difference between a Scottish and a Liverpudlian accent quite easily, for example.

Inflexion describes the way an individual pronounces certain words. For example, take a simple word like 'Hallo'. Some people say it with the emphasis on the first part: '*Ha*-llo'. Someone else might say it with the emphasis on the second part: 'Ha-*llo*'. Getting something as simple as this right may make all the difference to your impression.

Perfect accents

Good impressionists have an ear for accents. They only have to hear a few phrases of a Newcastle or Welsh accent and they're immediately able to speak in the manner of someone else. If you can do that you're lucky – and if not, and if you still can't quite capture an accent after listening to it dozens of times, try writing it down. Don't just jot down the words; write them the way they are pronounced by the person you want to imitate. Forget everything you've ever learned about spelling – invent new spellings that describe the way they sound!

Here's a quick example of how an American accent could look written down: 'Hi ya'wl! Mah name's J.R. and ah cuurm frum Sowth Fawk in Daallas'.

A posh southern accent might look like this:

15

'Hell-o, mi naim is Queen Elizabeth II and Ai live in Buckinghem Pelece.'

Now try reading back what you've written. It should help you get the vowels and the inflexions sorted out – though it may do terrible damage to your spelling skills!

Hearing yourself speak

We very rarely hear ourselves as others hear us. I remember the first time I heard myself on a tape recorder and thought, 'I'm sure I don't really sound like that'. Hearing your voice as others do can be a great surprise! The reason why we sound one way to ourselves and quite different to other people is because of the way in which our own voice travels directly back to our ears.

To find out what you sound like to the rest of the world, take two books and place their spines against the side of your head just in front of your ears. Now count to ten. You will probably discover that your voice is slightly higher in pitch and less strong than you thought it was! The books work by preventing the sound passing straight back to your ears; instead, you hear what everyone else hears.

When you think you have perfected someone else's voice try the book test and see if it still sounds like the person you're attempting to imitate. If it does, well done!

Noisy impressions

As I said at the beginning of this chapter, you can do a lot of impressions based on a sound alone – your impressions don't have to be of people. Try a couple of these for a giggle:

The Buzzing Fly: This noise is ideal for playing practical jokes on people. Once you've got the hang of it you will be able to convince them that there's a horrible bluebottle buzzing around their head!

Press your lips together quite tightly. Now force air out through them so that the centre of your lips vibrate and make a high-pitched buzz. If you find it difficult, try licking your lips and keep practising until you can make a convincing buzzing!

Frog Croak: Normally while we talk we breathe out. When we've used all our breath we stop talking, take another breath and start again. By breathing in while you talk you can develop a very strange voice that doesn't sound like you at all, and you can also do some excellent impressions. How about a frog imitation? Say 'nee-dip' breathing in as you speak. Repeat it several times until it sounds like a frog croaking!

The Cat Fight: Be careful where you do this impression! If you try it in the garden at night

17

you may find someone throws a bucket of cold water over you!

Place your tongue against your top teeth and make a quiet 'sssss' noise, like a hissing snake. Gradually increase it in volume until you're out of breath. Then say 'ree-yow!' in a high, nasal voice that tails off into a squeal several times. Allow a few seconds of silence so that people think that cats have gone their separate ways and then start all over again!

The Bottle Pop and Pour: Drive your friends crazy by asking if they'd like a drink, then going into the kitchen and doing this impression:

To make the noise of the cork being pulled

from the bottle, place the tip of your index finger in your mouth with the back of your hand towards your face. Seal your lips around the finger and fill your cheeks with air by breathing through your nose. Now snap your finger out, catching the corner of your mouth as you do so. It should make a convincing 'pop' noise. Keep practising until you can make a really loud and impressive pop!

Now for the 'glug glug' sound as you pour the imaginary drinks from the bottle. To make this noise shape your mouth as if you were saying 'O'. Breath through your nose and as you do so tap the side of your cheek (which should feel quite taut) with one finger. It should make a hollow kind of noise and you can vary the pitch and volume by tapping in different spots and more or less firmly. String together a few of these hollow tapping noises to make a 'glug glug glug glug' sound.

GARY'S VOICE CHECK CHALLENGE!

Test your skill at vocal impressions with some voice check challenges. Can you imitate these famous people's catch-phrases and styles of talking? If you don't already know what they sound like, watch out for them on TV!

GARY'S VOICE CHECK CHALLENGE 1

How good are you at imitating comedian Michael Barrymore? Try his famous catch-phrase – 'All right!'

GARY'S VOICE CHECK CHALLENGE 2

Boxing fans should find this one easy. Have a go at copying boxer Frank Bruno saying: 'It was a good fight, Harry'.

GARY'S VOICE CHECK CHALLENGE 3

Who's the greatest rodent megastar the universe has ever known? Roland Rat of course! If you're a fan, you shouldn't have any difficulty doing an impression of Roland saying: 'Greetings, Ratfans, 'tis I, the one and only Roland! *Yeahhhhh!*'

GARY'S VOICE CHECK CHALLENGE 4

It's not too difficult to do a vocal impression of Norman Wisdom. Have a go yourself. All you have to do is go 'Wey-ay-hey-ay' – but with the right accent and inflexion!

GARY'S VOICE CHECK CHALLENGE 5

You may not be able to do magic tricks but can you say 'You're going to like this – not a lot' like Paul Daniels?

GARY'S VOICE CHECK CHALLENGE 6

Try imitating one of the most famous British screen actors around at the moment by saying, 'My name is Michael Caine' as Michael Caine himself might say it.

WATCH CLOSELY

Some people think that the most important thing of all when it comes to doing impressions is looking exactly like the person you are imitating – but I'm pleased to say that's not true, otherwise I wouldn't be able to do many impressions! As I've found, you can do a good impression of Madonna or Diana Ross or Norman Wisdom, for a few examples, without looking much like them.

The most important thing is to get the voice right. After that, you can work on perfecting the gestures and facial expressions of your subject. After all, Stevie Wonder wouldn't be Stevie Wonder if he didn't roll his head from side to side in his characteristic manner, and I can't imagine doing my impression of Norman Wisdom without all the movements and gestures to match! So, if you're going to do a really good impression of someone, anyone from your Mum to Mrs Thatcher, take some time to watch closely.

Movement and expression/ Using video tapes

Whenever I'm asked how I decide which characters to do impressions of, I have to be honest and say that most of them just come to me. I like doing people with interesting faces and expressions – I watch them, and the next thing I know I'm doing an impression of them! A few years ago, though, I was part of a TV show called *Copy Cats* which was a programme solely of impressions. I had to learn quite a lot of new characters quickly, and I discovered that using a video tape was a good way of studying someone and copying their movements and expressions. If you find that you're having difficulty perfecting an impression and you're lucky enough to have a video recorder you can make a tape of the person you want to impersonate in action and then play it back over and over again until you get it right.

Start by mastering your character's facial expressions. Then add his or her hand movements before studying and copying the way they walk. By the time you've done all this you'll only need to add the voice and you'll have an excellent impression!

If you don't have a video recorder you'll have to watch your subject on television or in films. To help you remember their gestures and movements why not jot down a few notes or sketches to remind yourself of the things they do? Keep practising your impression until you get it right. Ask other people to watch you rehearsing and see if they can guess who you are simply by your movements and expression. This may sound a tall order but there are a surprising number of people whose looks and actions are so individual that you don't have to say a word to do a great impression of them. Here are a few challenges I'd like you to have a go at:

Michael Barrymore – be careful you don't hurt yourself if you copy the way he walks!

Groucho Marx – to walk like Groucho bend your whole body forward, put your left hand in the middle of your back with the palm facing outwards and pretend to hold in front of you, in your right hand, a large cigar. Take very long steps and raise and lower your eyebrows all the while.

Norman Wisdom – wey-ey-hey-ay!

David Bellamy – throw your arms around wildly and look very enthusiastic about things.

Max Bygraves – you don't have to sing, just dangle your hands!

The Vicious Boys – make sure you don't damage the furniture when you do this one . . .

These are a little more difficult but not impossible to do silently:

Les Dawson – ideal for those people with false teeth that they can take out but more difficult for everyone else!

Griff Rhys Jones – try hunching your shoulders and dancing from foot to foot while looking as if you've just done something very silly.

Mavis from *Coronation Street* – simply look shy and keep putting your head on one side.

Rod Hull and Emu – keep your right arm bent with your hand at shoulder height. This represents Emu. Thrust your right hand out and throw the rest of your body after it, as if your arm was trying to escape. Go round chasing and pinching the audience until they scream!

Once you've got these impressions down to a tee, keep practising. I do – in the car. It gets a bit embarrassing when other people see me at it, but it probably makes someone's day, seeing a barmy bloke talking to himself in the rear-view mirror!

MAKING FACES

I don't use very much make-up for my impressions because I like to think that it really doesn't matter whether you look much like the character you're impersonating or not. In fact it's sometimes much more funny if you *don't* look like the character, so long as you get the voice and the gestures right! And of course, when I do my live act, I don't have time to go away and change my make-up for each character.

However, if you're going to a fancy dress party you'll want to look as much like your chosen personality as possible. So this chapter is about using make-up and special effects to change the way you look and transform your features.

Your make-up kit

First of all you'll need to put together a basic make-up kit. If you want to look fairly natural – for example, if you have been invited to a fancy dress party – it's best to use ordinary make-up of the kind you can buy from most department stores and chemist shops. If you want to make a more theatrical impression and you're not worried about looking realistic you can use coloured face paints, the sort which come in crayon-shaped sticks. You'll find them on sale in many toy shops and they shouldn't be too expensive.

MOVIE STAR MAKE-UP

You can use this make-up for any glamorous female character from Madonna to Alexis! Before you start, study the kind of colours your character wears and the shape of her face, eyebrows and lips. Then by following these steps and incorporating her 'look' you can make your face give: The Right Impression!

1 Dot a little foundation on your cheeks, nose, forehead and chin and smooth it gently over your skin. Use a slightly damp piece of cotton wool to spread it evenly. If you're using face paints, blend them in with your fingers.

2 Dust your face with powder or with a little talcum powder on a piece of cotton wool. Remove excess powder with more cotton wool.

3 Use shader, highlighter and blusher to change the shape of your face. The shader can slim your cheeks, the highlighter draws attention to your cheekbones, and the blusher gives your face colour. The diagrams show where to use them for the best effect.

4 Using a brown or black eye pencil or crayon,

shade in your eyebrows with short, light strokes until they are the same shape as your character's eyebrows.

CHANGING THE SHAPE OF YOUR FACE

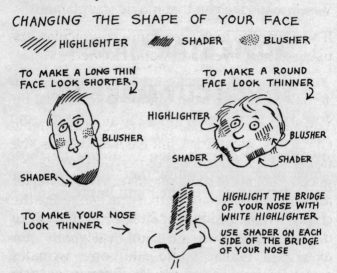

///// HIGHLIGHTER   ///// SHADER   ∷∷ BLUSHER

TO MAKE A LONG THIN
FACE LOOK SHORTER

BLUSHER

SHADER

TO MAKE A ROUND
FACE LOOK THINNER

HIGHLIGHTER

BLUSHER

SHADER

SHADER

TO MAKE YOUR NOSE
LOOK THINNER →

HIGHLIGHT THE BRIDGE
OF YOUR NOSE WITH
WHITE HIGHLIGHTER

USE SHADER ON EACH
SIDE OF THE BRIDGE
OF YOUR NOSE

5 Colour your lids with eyeshadow or crayon and blend it in.

6 Draw a fine pencil line along the upper and lower lid, close to the lashes. Smudge it with a piece of damp cotton wool so that it doesn't look too thick. Blend a little highlighter or white crayon just under the eyebrows. Finish your eyes off with mascara.

7 Apply the lipstick or crayon to your mouth. If you want to change the shape of your mouth to make the lips wider or thicker or thinner, draw the outline *first* using a very fine brush. Dab the brush on the lipstick, then carefully draw in the new shape. When you have got it right, fill in the outline. Finish off with plenty of lip gloss or Vaseline to give you that movie star glamour!

If you want to look even more spectacular, try using glittery eyeshadow and blusher!

TOUGH GUY MAKE-UP

You can use this make-up for all sorts of male characters, including Clint Eastwood and some not-so-tough guys too. Before you start, take a good long look at some photos of your character and at your own face so that you can judge the changes that need to be made. If you're going to do an impression of Clint Eastwood, for example, you'll need to add some wrinkles around your eyes and mouth. If you want to do an impression of Bob Geldof don't make your face too tanned but be sure to add plenty of designer stubble around your chin!

If you've chosen a character with a beard or moustache you can either go along to a shop specialising in theatrical costumes and make-up and buy a false beard or moustache or you can cheat and just draw one in!

1 Apply foundation by dotting it on your cheeks, nose, chin and forehead and blending it in with your fingers or a piece of damp cotton wool. If the character you're impersonating has a tan use a dark shade of foundation or mix some brown face paint with the flesh-coloured crayon to give yourself a weatherbeaten look. Remember to smooth the foundation down your neck so that it doesn't look as if you have a dirty tide-mark around your chin!

2 Use the highlighter and shader to shape your chin and cheeks if necessary. Follow the diagrams on page 28 to get the right effect.

3 If your character has deep-set eyes, use the brown shader on your eyelids. With your black eye pencil draw a fine line along your upper lashes and smudge it in using your finger or a piece of cotton wool.

4 Add 'stubble' around your chin by dotting with the black or brown pencil and rubbing it in with your finger to give your skin a greyish or dark look. Then, using a sharp-tipped pencil, draw a few fine black dots and tiny lines to represent the bristles.

5 For wrinkles draw a fine line with the brown pencil. If it's a deep-looking wrinkle, draw a *fine* white stripe close under it and smudge it so that it fades out. This will highlight the wrinkle.

6 For a nasty-looking scar draw a fine red or brown line across your cheek or chin. Fade it out at the end using your fingers. Paint a narrow white stripe down each side of the scar.

Smudge it slightly. Finish off by drawing red or brown dots in pairs down the length of the scar. These represent the marks left by the stitches that once held the cut together!

7 If you think you need some colour, add a *little* red blusher or crayon to the centre of each cheek. Now all you have to do is act as tough as you look!

WRINKLY MAKE-UP

You can use this make-up, and variations on it, to do impressions of all sorts of people, from Ethel of *EastEnders* fame to Super Gran! In fact *anyone* who's going grey and has a few wrinkles. As with the other make-ups, try to study your character's face before you start so that you know what kind of colours and shapes to aim for.

1 Make up your face with a pale foundation unless your chosen character has a dark skin tone (in which case, copy them). Smooth foundation over your face and neck and set it with a dusting of powder, as before.

2 Sitting in front of a mirror, do your impression. Pull the faces that your character makes and notice where your skin wrinkles while you're doing so. If your character looks very gloomy, you'll probably notice that you're get-

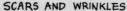

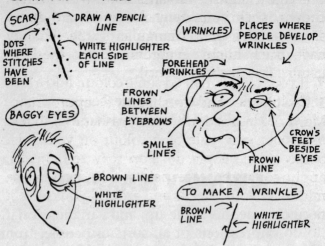

SCARS AND WRINKLES

SCAR — DRAW A PENCIL LINE

DOTS WHERE STITCHES HAVE BEEN

WHITE HIGHLIGHTER EACH SIDE OF LINE

WRINKLES — PLACES WHERE PEOPLE DEVELOP WRINKLES

FOREHEAD WRINKLES

FROWN LINES BETWEEN EYEBROWS

BAGGY EYES

SMILE LINES

CROW'S FEET BESIDE EYES

FROWN LINE

BROWN LINE

WHITE HIGHLIGHTER

TO MAKE A WRINKLE

BROWN LINE

WHITE HIGHLIGHTER

ting slight vertical lines from your nose down to your mouth. If your character laughs a lot, he or she will probably have laughter lines by their eyes and mouth. Some characters just have wrinkles beneath their eyes. Trace in these lines with a sharp-tipped brown pencil and smudge them slightly at each end. *Don't* cover your face with too many wrinkles or you'll end up looking like a map!

3 If your character has very deep wrinkles or frown lines, emphasise them with a narrow white highlight. If the wrinkle runs horizontally, put the white line underneath and smudge it in slightly. If the wrinkle runs vertically, put a narrow stripe of white at each side and rub it in.

4 If your character has a thin face with sunken cheeks, suck your own cheeks in and apply some shader in a triangular shape. If they have thick bushy eyebrows, draw these in using a fine eyebrow pencil.

5 Use blusher and eyeshadow as appropriate. Many old ladies don't wear eyeshadow, so just use some very pale blue colour on your lids. Some older people develop rosy red cheeks; apply some red face paint or lipstick in the middle of your cheeks and around your nose if necessary.

HORROR MAKE-UP

This make-up is ideal for playing Count Dracula or other spooks – and also for Charlie Chaplin, Groucho Marx and other characters from black and white films! It looks best if you use children's face paints or professional stage make-up.

1 Instead of using flesh-coloured foundation, cover your face with the white face paint. Cover your lips and eyebrows with it too. It already looks quite spooky, doesn't it!

2 If you're going to play Count Dracula, shade carefully under your cheekbones with grey crayon. Use this around your eyes, too, to give them a horrible sunken look, and trace a few wrinkles and lines around the mouth.

3 Now for your eyebrows! Experiment with drawing in new, bushy black eyebrows above your own. Try different shapes. You can imitate Groucho Marx by drawing rough rectangular ones. Groucho moves his eyebrows up and down a lot and by positioning your new brows in the right spot you can achieve a really good effect. Charlie Chaplin had little curved black eyebrows, and his eyes were ringed with a line of black crayon.

EYEBROWS

GROUCHO MARX   CHARLIE CHAPLIN

4 To give yourself a very long, thin-looking nose, shade the sides of your nose with pale grey crayon and draw an arrow shape at the tip.

5 If you want to look really horrific, you can go crazy and draw in lots of shadows, wrinkles and warts! Try using touches of pale green and violet colour under your eyes and on your lips or to highlight your forehead or chin. Finish off with a dusting of ghostly talcum powder to 'set' your whole face. You'll end up looking absolutely horrible!

Taking make-up off

It's important that you get every scrap of make-up off your face, otherwise you may develop spots! If you've got lots of greasy face paints or stage make-up on, begin by wiping your face with a tissue and taking off the top layer. Then massage some cream cleanser into your skin – baby lotion or cold cream will do perfectly. Using more clean tissues or cotton wool, continue wiping it away. Keep doing this until *all* the make-up has come off, then wash your face with mild soap and water and dry it carefully. If after all this your skin feels dry, smooth in some moisturiser.

Changing your hair

Most professional impressionists use wigs and hairpieces in their work, but wigs are expensive and sometimes difficult to find. You can change the colour of your hair for a day or two by using a wash in-wash out hair colour. These work best if you want to make your hair darker – if you want to turn your hair from blonde to brown, for example – and they should disappear after a few shampoos. You can also get coloured styling mousse which will give your hair a red or blue or brown tint. It's probably best to check with Mum and Dad though *before* you change the colour of your hair!

Some specialist theatrical shops and large chemists sell coloured sprays which you can use on your hair like ordinary hairspray and which wash out afterwards. Among the colours they offer are black and silver. The silver is useful for creating grey streaks in your hair if you're doing an impression of an elderly person. Another method of achieving this effect is to dust your hair with talcum powder. Don't overdo it though! If you do, you'll leave a cloud of talc floating behind you wherever you go!

When it comes to changing the style of your hair, you can do almost anything with modern styling gels and mousses. You can slick your hair back to your head with gel. If you've got straight hair and you want tumbling curls, brush plenty of styling mousse through dry hair and then set it on rollers or, better still, around the new soft fabric hair curlers.

To achieve a punk style with your hair on end, wash it and then give it a good slick of setting gel. Blow dry it into the style you want, making sure that you dry the hair right down to the roots. Add more styling gel or mousse if necessary. So that you're absolutely certain it will stay in place give it a good squirt of hair-spray or, even better, special fixing spray which is far stronger than ordinary hairspray.

To achieve a bouffant, fluffy style, take a lock of hair and comb it gradually in the wrong direction; from the tip of the hair down to the root. This is called back-combing and it builds up body and makes your hair look like a fluffy cloud. However, it's not advisable to do this too often as it can cause very bad split ends.

If, after all this, you still don't feel that your face and hair look exactly like the person you want to impersonate, don't worry. Forget all about your hair and make-up and concentrate on all the other things that go to make your subject so distinctive instead. Remember, most impressionists don't rely too much on make-up and props. Take it from me that it's the other things like voice, gestures and stories, that are the most important when it comes to making a good impression!

FAMOUS IMPRESSIONS

Some of these impressions are perfect if you're invited to a fancy dress party or you want to do a really close impression of a star. It's great fun dressing up, and I've always found that a lot of the enjoyment comes from making my own props. I used to spend hours making the costumes for my impressions and I still make most of my own accessories, including false moustaches and wigs and things.

Anyone can spend a lot of money on buying the perfect outfit and props but it's really not necessary. In fact, it takes away a lot of the fun of getting an act together. Years ago I used to do an impression of Idi Amin, who was in the

news at the time. He used to wear a military jacket and cap and lots of medals pinned to his chest. Rather than go out and buy everything, I found an old blue jacket of my father's. I cut the sleeves off and made a military-style cap from one of them. Then I made dozens of medals out of milk bottle tops and crepe paper. It looked really funny – much funnier than if I'd spent a fortune on real medals!

And another thing. Remember that you don't actually need to look anything like Adrian Mole or Stevie Wonder to do brilliant impressions of them! It's just the illusion that counts, honestly! In fact I believe that anyone can do an impression of almost anyone else, no matter what they look like. If I come across someone I can't imitate accurately then I just go over the top, which makes the impression even more funny. Take Humphrey Bogart, for example. Now I don't look anything like Humphrey Bogart, so instead of trying to get him right I deliberately do him wrong and wear a blond wig that makes me look like Shirley Temple! It sounds crazy but it works, and it makes the impression much funnier than it would be if I spent hours trying to apply make-up and wigs in an attempt to look exactly like him.

Of all the impressions I do, Stevie Wonder is my favourite. I made the outfit for him myself. It's so simple that you could do it too! First I took a pair of dark glasses and attached a piece

of black elastic to the arms so that they didn't
fall off when I was wearing them. Then I sus-
pended strands of black wool over the arms of
the glasses and all round the elastic at the back
and tied them in place. The final touch is some
coloured beads threaded onto the wool 'hair'
and it's finished. You just slip the glasses on
with elastic around your head and there you are
– Stevie Wonder! You can complete the impression by singing one of his songs and
waggling your head from side to side in his
distinctive manner. And don't worry if the rest
of your hair is blond, it'll just be even funnier!

The singer Randy Crawford is another
favourite of mine. Again, you can make your
own wig for an impression of her using a piece
of elastic and wool or fine strips of crepe paper

or anything else that looks vaguely right. Find something nice and sparkly to wear, sing in a falsetto voice and you'll have another great success. I was once given a wonderful dress for Randy to wear, but unfortunately it was very low-cut at the front and showed my hairy chest. We tried to cover it with make-up but nothing worked, so in the end I had to shave my chest! I didn't mind, because I believe that you have to be prepared to try all kinds of things out to make a performance work.

You can experiment with the ideas in this chapter. Remember, you *don't* have to follow the guidelines exactly. Use your own fresh ideas to make even crazier impressions of your favourite famous people. And I hope you enjoy making all the costumes and props and getting dressed up just as much as I do!

ALEXIS FROM *DYNASTY*

The great thing about Alexis is that she looks so wonderfully glamorous but behaves so wickedly, getting herself into lots of scrapes, yet she is always saved at the last moment. If you want the chance to behave very, very badly, try impersonating her – though, unlike the real Alexis, I can't guarantee that you won't get into big trouble!

WHAT YOU NEED:

- ★ A big jacket
- ★ A tight skirt
- ★ High heels
- ★ A big hat
- ★ A belt
- ★ Two plastic cups
- ★ A piece of string (about 60cm long)
- ★ Hairspray
- ★ Vaseline
- ★ A dozen socks *or* a piece of garden cane about 75cm long
- ★ Lots of jewellery
- ★ Thin cardboard
- ★ Red felt pen
- ★ Sticky tape
- ★ Movie Star make-up (see page 27)
- ★ A desk or table with some papers on it
- ★ A telephone
- ★ A chair
- ★ A sofa
- ★ A mirror

PUTTING IT TOGETHER:

1 Cut out very long and pointed fingernail shapes from the cardboard. Colour them red with the felt pen and leave to dry.

2 Make up your face following the Movie Star guidelines on page 27 and making sure that you use plenty of red lipstick. Add a good slurp of Vaseline on top of the lipstick; Alexis always wears lots of lipgloss.

3 Using a brush and the hairspray, pile your hair up as high as it will go and fluff it out. Spray it so that it's really hard and shiny. If this doesn't work, tuck your hair up and wear the hat.

4 Tie each plastic cup to one end of the piece of string. Put the string around your neck so that the cups dangle in front of you. Adjust them so that your 'bosom' is in the right place.

5 Put on the skirt. Place the stick across the shoulders inside the jacket and put it on. If you're not using the stick, pad the shoulders of the jacket with the socks, until they're really huge!

6 Pin on as much jewellery as you can. Put the belt around the jacket and do it up so tightly you can hardly breathe. Tape the false nails to the end of your fingers – just wind a piece of tape over the nail and around your fingertip. Lastly, step into your high heels!

WHAT YOU DO:
1 Glide into the room. Sit elegantly at the desk. Look sideways, holding your chin up. Raise one eyebrow knowingly at the audience and give a wicked smile.

2 Pick up a piece of paper from the desk. Look at it briefly.

3 The telephone rings (ask someone to do the sound effect for you). Take off your ear-ring and pick up the receiver *very* delicately. If you want to get a laugh, hold the phone to the wrong ear!

4 Pretending to listen to someone at the other end of the phone, say very coolly; 'Alexis speaking . . . We *can* buy up the oil pipeline so that Blake will be ruined? . . . That is wonderful! . . . Ten million dollars? (Laugh) I'll pay anything to see Blake brought to his knees . . .' Put down the phone and give another wicked laugh.

5 Stand up, pick up the piece of paper and walk to the sofa. Sit down. Cross your legs very elegantly but make sure that everyone can see several inches of thigh.

6 Say, with your chin in the air and a malicious smile on your face, 'So, Blake and Krystle, you're in for a nasty surprise. I shall have my revenge! By the time I've finished you'll be out on the street with no money, no family, no friends . . . *Nothing!!*'

Take the sheet of paper and rip it very neatly in two. Drop the bits on the floor as if they were something nasty. Stand up. Throw back your head and give your very wickedest laugh, then turn and leave the room. At this point, if you're playing it for laughs you could trip over or bump into the doorway!

EASTENDERS VARIATION: This make-up and outfit can also be used to impersonate Angie from *EastEnders*! Don't wear the hat but do use extra eye-shadow so that you look as if you have two black eyes. Substitute a Cockney accent, laugh hysterically all the time and say things like, 'You all right, darlin'?'

JIMMY CRICKET

If English people tell Irish jokes, Irish people quite understandably object. The *only* way to tell Irish jokes and not get into trouble is to be Irish yourself, like Jimmy Cricket. Here's what to do!

WHAT YOU NEED:

★ Large black jacket (if you can find an evening jacket with tails it will be ideal)
★ Black trousers
★ Extra-large pair of wellington boots
★ Large black hat, preferably made of felt
★ White shirt
★ Black bow tie or black ribbon about 2cm wide and 60cm long
★ A flower for a buttonhole
★ Cotton wool or small piece of clean foam rubber
★ Paper
★ Black felt pen
★ Glue
★ A letter in an envelope
★ A friend in the audience

PUTTING IT TOGETHER:

1 Fold the tops of your wellies inside out. Cut out large letters R and L from the paper and colour them black. Using glue (preferably the sort that will wash off later) stick them on to the folded-over parts.

2 If you need to make your cheeks look more full pad them out with a piece of cotton wool or foam rubber. Make sure you don't swallow it!

3 Put on the shirt and the bow tie. If you don't have a bow tie, use the black ribbon to make one. Put on the trousers and roll them up to just below the knee. Put on the jacket and pin the flower to the lapel. Pull the hat on so that it comes to your eyebrows. Make sure the brim is well down.

4 Put the wellingtons on the wrong feet and the letter in your pocket.

WHAT YOU DO:

1 First of all, practise Jimmy Cricket's grin and Irish accent. When you've got them sorted out, you're ready to go.

2 Walk into the room backwards. Turn round, look surprised, give a big grin and wave.

3 Go up to the audience. Grin. Beckon with your finger and say, 'Come here,' remembering your Irish accent. Repeat this a couple of times. Keep grinning!

4 Say: 'You know, I heard from my Mammy a couple of days ago that the Irish have cracked the Green Cross Code. But they say there's no need to worry. They're going to get it fixed again.'

5 With a bit of luck people will laugh at this. Then say: 'And there's more!' Grin again. Take out the letter and unfold it. Say: 'I've just had a letter all the way from Ireland, from my Mammy. She's been having a very busy time. Shall I read what she says? Shall I?' At this point your friend in the audience should yell 'Yes!'

6 Grin some more. Read the letter: 'This is what my Mammy wrote. She said, "Dear Son" – that's me, you know – "On Monday I had all my teeth out and Mr Kelly came and installed a new washing-machine."' Grin at the audience. '"On Tuesday I knitted a pair of socks for your cousin Brendan but I don't think they'll fit him because he's grown another foot."' Grin again. '"On Wednesday I had Mrs O'Reilly for lunch. She was very nice."' Grin some more. '"Please excuse my handwriting, son. I am writing quickly so that I can finish your letter before the ink in the pen runs out. Your loving Mammy. P.S. Next Saturday afternoon we're going on a picnic, unless it rains, in which case we'll go in the morning." Aah, isn't it nice to get a letter from your Mammy?' Grin!

7 Say: 'I've got to go now. I've got an appoint-
ment with the chiropodist. My fate (pronounced like feet) is in his hands! Goodbye!'

CLINT EASTWOOD

If you're not very good at accents and you don't
like telling jokes, have a go at impersonating
Clint Eastwood. He doesn't have much to say –
he just looks tough!

WHAT YOU NEED:
★ A cowboy-style hat with a wide brim
★ An old blanket or poncho
★ Coloured felt pens
★ A dark-coloured shirt
★ A belt (if you don't have a gun holster)
★ A square scarf or piece of plain fabric about 60cm square
★ Tough guy make-up (see page 29)
★ Toy gun with exploding caps and holster

PUTTING IT TOGETHER:
1 Make your face up in the Tough Guy style
on page 29. Using a brown eyebrow pencil
draw some lines from the outer corner of each
eye; this is because Clint has developed
wrinkles from screwing up his eyes in the
sun.

2 Put on your dark-coloured shirt, fold the
scarf or square of fabric in half diagonally and

tie it around your neck. Sling your holster around your hips or put on the belt and stick the gun through it.

3 If you're using a poncho, put it on. If you've got an old blanket fold it in half. Measure the length from your shoulder to just above your knee, mark the distance from the fold and carefully cut off the extra fabric. (Make sure you *can* cut the blanket *before* you start.) Now lift the top half of the blanket and cut a straight line up the middle to the fold. If you want you can decorate the blanket with some felt pen squiggles before you put it on.

4 Put on the hat and pull it down until it meets your eyebrows. Do you feel really mean yet?

WHAT YOU DO:
1 Screw up your eyes tightly, as if you've been looking at the sun for a long time. Clench your back teeth together, then pull back your lips to show all your teeth.

2 Now you're ready to do your imitation. Walk across the room very slowly, looking from one person to the next with complete contempt. Remember to keep your eyes screwed up like slits.

3 Clench your teeth in a menacing smile and pull the brim of your hat down, all the time watching people.

4 Throw one half of your poncho/blanket over the opposite shoulder, then turn around and walk slowly out using long strides.

5 Walk out the door, count to five, then come slowly back in for a few paces and say in the deepest, meanest voice you can manage: 'Did somebody say something?' Let your hand hover over your gun. If there is total silence, turn round and walk out again. If anyone speaks, shoot them with your cap gun and make a dignified exit.

BEN VOLPELIERE-PIERROT

Do you want to be a pop star? Then why not have a go at an impression of brilliant Ben Volpeliere-Pierrot of Curiosity Killed the Cat. If you're any good at it you could win yourself some fans!

WHAT YOU NEED:
- ★ A haircut
- ★ Hair gel
- ★ A black beret
- ★ A black shirt or zip-up jacket
- ★ Black jeans or trousers
- ★ Black plimsolls or other black shoes
- ★ A chunk of Blu-Tack or something similar
- ★ A cardboard tube from a toilet roll
- ★ A ping-pong ball painted black
- ★ Silver paper
- ★ Glue

★ A Curiosity Killed the Cat tape and something to play it on *or* your personal backing band. (It's best to use a tape if you're dancing close by. You can bump into a record player and scratch the record if you're not careful.)

★ Table lamps and torches

★ Lighting assistants

PUTTING IT TOGETHER:

1 The day before you want to do this impression, go and have a haircut. Your hair should be very short at the back and sides.

2 Cover the toilet roll tube with silver paper and glue the black ping-pong ball to one end. This will be your microphone!

3 Slick back what is left of your hair with the gel. Stick a few bits of Blu-Tack behind your ears to make them stick out. (If you've already got sticky-out ears you can forget this stage!)

4 Put on the black jeans. Put on your shirt and do up *all* the buttons, including the one at the neck. If you're wearing a zip-up jacket, zip it all the way to the top.

5 Put on the beret and pull well down. Any badges or decoration should be worn at the back.

WHAT YOU DO:

1 Decide which song you are going to sing and memorise the words so that you can mime to them. If you have friends who can play music well, get them to learn the song while you practise singing it for real.

2 If you have access to a video recorder, make a tape of Ben in action so that you can study the way he dances and his gestures. The basic movement you have to master is the 'wobbly-leg' dance! See the diagrams below.

Stand with your feet about 30cm apart and leaning forward. Position A: turn your feet out and bend slightly at the knees so that they point outwards, too. You can throw your arms wide at this point. Now turn your toes and knees inwards and hunch down slightly, bringing

BEN VOLPELIERE-PIERROT

POSITION A

POSITION B

your arms in so that you're in position B. That's the basic movement; if you do it fast enough it makes your legs look as if they are made of rubber and as if you're about to fall over! Once you have the hang of it you'll be able to do it while you are bouncing around.

3 To make your impersonation look exciting, organise some lighting effects. Find as many table lamps, reading lamps and torches as you can and put a friend in charge of each of them. You can buy coloured lightbulbs from an electrical shop to give a brilliant display and for the torches you can stretch coloured plastic sweet wrappings over the glass (Quality Street is ideal for this!). Station your friends around the 'stage' area with their lamps and get them to switch them on and off as you dance around. Get one person to aim their torch at your feet, another at your face, and so on. Get everyone to practise this together and develop some special effects – dancing with a bright light shining behind you, for example, can look very good.

4 Before you make your entrance get your friends into position, then switch the lights off. Start the tape, make your appearance with the lights flashing, sing the song and make a quick exit before your fans can grab you!

COMEDY EXTRA: If you'd like to make your impression funny, don't sing a Curiosity Killed the Cat song. Try to find something that no one would expect to hear Ben Volpeliere-Pierrot sing and then do it in his style. How about 'Knees Up, Mother Brown'? Or write some new and funny words and put them to one of his tunes!

ADRIAN MOLE

Adrian Mole is the most famous 13¾-year-old in Britain – but fortunately you don't have to be exactly 13¾ years old to do a good impression of him. This impression works best if you have dark hair and spots. Yes, spots! They can be faked but this is one impression where real spots are a great advantage.

WHAT YOU NEED:
★ Smart school uniform including blazer *or*
★ If you're blond, substitute a parka or anorak with a hood for the blazer
★ Large black briefcase
★ Red socks
★ Glasses – preferably the round, swotty-looking type
★ Hair gel
★ Rice Krispies
★ Spirit gum or Blu-Tack
★ Diary or notebook
★ Paper, coloured felt pens, glue
★ A copy of *The Secret Diary of Adrian Mole aged 13¾*

PUTTING IT TOGETHER:

1 On sheets of paper write the words SECRET DIARY. Colour the letters and then cut them out and stick them to the front of the note-book or diary. When it's finished, put it in the briefcase.

2 If you already suffer from spots you can miss out this stage, but if you have good skin you're going to have to add some blemishes. Take a Rice Krispie and carefully cut it in half. Using a red felt pen put a few dots of colour on the rounded side. Make several 'spots' like this. Now, using spirit gum or false eyelash glue or tiny pieces of Blu-Tack rolled into the 'spot', stick them on around your chin and forehead. *Yuck!*

3 Dab some hair gel on your hair and comb it through so that it looks as if it's greasy. Put on the glasses.

4 Get into school uniform, and add the red socks. If you're a blond Adrian Mole put on the parka or anorak and put the hood up so that it hugs your face.

5 Practise a Birmingham-style accent and trudging along with your head down, carrying the briefcase as if it was terribly heavy.

WHAT YOU DO:

1 If you haven't already done so, read *The Secret Diary of Adrian Mole*. Get to know the characters and their habits.

2 Walk around with your hand over your chin to hide your spots and keep pushing your glasses back up your nose.

3 Walk into the room or arrive at the party in a terrible hurry, as if you're late. Say: 'Hello, I'm Adrian Mole. I'm sorry I'm late but I've just had a dead awful experience. Bert Baxter ran out of jars of beetroot so I took his alsatian dog, Sabre, down to Sainsbury's. I'd got the beetroot and I was just standing in the queue waiting to pay for it when a woman came racing in and said, "Who owns the alsatian dog tied up outside?"

"He's with me," I told her. I thought Sabre must have bitten her or something.

"I've got some bad news," she said. "My dog's just killed him."

"What kind of dog have you got?" I asked. It would have to be something massive to kill Sabre.

"It's a poodle," she said.

"How did a poodle kill an alsatian?"

"He tried to eat it and it got stuck in his throat and choked him to death."

'Anyway, I've got to go away now and write it all down in my diary . . .' Take out your diary from the briefcase, wave it and make your exit.

4 If you're at a party, spend all your time talking about your undying adoration for Pandora and the problems you're having with your spots/dog/mother/father. You can also talk about how you are menaced at school by Barry Kent and discuss the state of the Belgian leather industry (Adrian Mole is an expert on this subject). If there is a mirror in the room, go up to it every few minutes and check your spots. Ask everyone else what they use on *their* spots!

MADONNA

Madonna changes her image and her hair colour so often that it's difficult to keep up with her. Whatever she wears, though, she's very distinctive – and that's good news for budding impressionists. There are two ways of looking like Madonna, depending on whether you're dark-haired or blonde . . .

DARK MADONNA

WHAT YOU NEED:

- ★ An assortment of trendy clothing, including a cut off sleeveless T-shirt, a mini-skirt, jeans, leggings etc.
- ★ Odd pieces of fabric, lace, ribbons etc.
- ★ Lots of bangles and beads
- ★ One lace glove
- ★ Hairspray
- ★ Black eyebrow pencil
- ★ Movie Star make-up (see page 27)
- ★ Tape of 'Like A Virgin' or 'Material Girl'
- ★ Tape recorder
- ★ Lighting display (see details in the Ben Volpeliere-Pierrot section, page 53)

PUTTING IT TOGETHER:

1 Spray and scrunch your hair into a wild mass, then take a piece of net or fabric, fold it into a headband and tie it round your head and into a bow at the front.

2 Finish the movie-star make-up with plenty of red lipstick. Take the eyebrow pencil and give yourself a beauty spot on the right side of your mouth, just below your nose.

3 From all your bits and pieces, put together an outfit. Make sure you have a couple of inches of bare midriff on show!

4 Put on all the bangles and wind the beads around your wrists to make more bracelets. Put on the lace glove.

WHAT YOU DO:

1 If you have access to a video recorder, get hold of a video of Madonna when she was first famous. Watch it carefully and copy her dance routines. If you can't do this, work up a suitable dance routine yourself!

2 Memorise the words of the song you have chosen and practise miming to it.

3 Practise pouting in front of the mirror. Put your right hand to your cheek and place your fourth and little finger on your lower lip. Press down slightly so that your teeth show. Stare moodily into the middle distance and throw your head back.

4 Organise your performance and rehearse it, with friends operating lamps and torches to give a good effect. (See page 53 for ideas for this.)

PLATINUM MADONNA

The new sophisticated blonde Madonna is a more difficult look to imitate. Why not use these ideas for dressing up like Madonna for a fancy dress party rather than for doing a close impression? And of course, it's far easier to look like today's Madonna if you're very blonde.

WHAT YOU NEED:

★ Shortish hair
★ Slinky dress (try your local jumble sales and Oxfam shops) *or*
★ Old-fashioned shiny satin petticoat (ask your grandmother if she has one!) *or*
★ Spanish fancy dress outfit *or*
★ Plain black or white leotard and leggings *plus*
★ 4m of black or white nylon net or chiffon fabric 150cm wide

★ Enough elastic to go easily round your waist
★ Talcum power
★ Hair gel
★ Black eyebrow pencil
★ Movie Star make-up (see page 27)
★ A friend who looks like Sean Penn
★ Two strong friends dressed as policemen

PUTTING IT TOGETHER:

1 If you can't find a slinky dress or a glamorous old-fashioned petticoat or a Spanish dancer's outfit, see if you can lay hands on a plain leotard and matching leggings. Buy 4m of nylon net fabric to match. Fold the net in half widthways, so that you have a double length of net 4m long and 75cm wide. Sew by hand or with a machine a line of stitching through both layers of net about 3cm beneath the fold.

Then sew the two ends of the net together to make a tube. Thread the elastic through the waistband, gathering the net up to make yourself a very full skirt. Sew the ends of the elastic together. Try the skirt on for length. If it is too long you can trim it. Why not cut a V-shaped pattern in the hem to make it look even more pretty?

2 Put on the Movie Star Make-up, varying it according to your outfit. If you have a very dark or very bright-coloured dress, use lots of red lipstick. If you're wearing a white leotard or pale dress use pale lipstick and eyeshadow and dust your whole face with talcum powder when you have finished. Using the black eyebrow pencil, add a beauty spot above the right side of your mouth, under the nose.

3 Using the hair gel, scrape back your hair and plaster it down so that it is completely flat and shiny. Or, if you prefer, use the gel on wet hair and blow dry it into Marilyn Monroe-style curls.

4 Put on your dress or the leotard and leggings with the net skirt over the top. Add some small touches of jewellery if you want to. Now you're ready for the party!

WHAT YOU DO:
1 Practise your poses! Walk slowly and elegantly, pointing your toes and with your shoul-

ders well back like a dancer. Stop. Look left, turning your face and chin so that they're parallel with your shoulder. Pout. Face the front again. Thrust your arms down at your sides and hold your head back with your chin up in the air. Pout again.

2 Every time someone tries to talk to you look sulky. The friend who is impersonating Sean Penn should step in at this point and pretend to start a fight. (No real fighting, please!) To make the whole impression perfect, friends dressed as policemen could then arrive and arrest him for causing trouble!

LUKE SKYWALKER AND DARTH VADER

Here's a hilarious impression for two friends to perform together. It's guaranteed to have your friends in stitches. You can take it in turns to be goodies and baddies!

WHAT YOU NEED:
For Luke Skywalker:

★ A white dressing gown (you can always turn a coloured one inside out)
or
★ A judo or karate outfit

★ A long piece of white material about 20cm wide and 200cm long *or* a wide white bandage
★ Safety pins
★ A belt

62

* ★ White plimsolls
* ★ A long torch

For Darth Vader:
* ★ A small stool about 50cm high
* ★ Lots of thick, shiny black bin liners
* ★ A piece of stick about 75cm long
* ★ String or tapes
* ★ A stapler
* ★ Black sticky tape *or* insulating tape
* ★ A cardboard box measuring approximately 45cm tall and 30cm wide and deep and painted shiny black
* ★ A long torch

Extra props:
* ★ A tape recorder playing the *Star Wars* theme
* ★ A friend to operate the tape recorder and say a few words

PUTTING IT TOGETHER:
Luke Skywalker

1 Put on the dressing gown or karate outfit.

2 Get someone to wind the strip of white fabric or bandage around you in a crossover shape. Finish off with safety pins.

3 Put the belt around your waist and stick the torch into it.

Darth Vader

1 Using a pair of scissors, cut three or four of the bin liners open so that you have flat

sheets of shiny black plastic. Stand on the stool and hold the piece of stick across your shoulders so that it sticks out at each side. Tie it in place using the string under your arms. Then find someone to help you make a kind of black plastic tent by hanging the bin bags over your shoulders and cutting and stapling them together until they reach the floor. You can hide any tears or obvious staples using the black sticky tape. If all this is too much bother, try to borrow a very large, shiny black plastic raincoat from someone and wear it buttoned up with the sleeves turned inside.

2 Put the torch in your pocket, under your 'cape'.

3 Put the cardboard box on your head. Cut three slits at the front so that you can see out. Where the box meets your shoulders, cut two semi-circles so that it fits properly.

4 Practise breathing heavily and speaking in a deep voice.

WHAT YOU DO:
1 Dim the lights. Play the *Star Wars* theme in the background. As it fades out Darth Vader comes on, puts down the stool, climbs onto it (making sure that it is covered by his cape) and moves his arms around as if he is striding along. (Don't try to run or you'll fall off the stool.) Breath very heavily.

2 Darth Vader cries: 'I know you are there, Luke Skywalker – I can feel the force. You must have had garlic for lunch.'

3 Enter Luke Skywalker behind Darth Vader. 'Here I am, Box Brain. Prepare to meet thy doom.'

4 Darth Vader breathes deeply and gurgles. 'You cannot kill me, Luke Skywalker.'

5 Luke Skywalker: 'Oh yes I can!' He leaps around and pulls out his torch. Darth Vader pulls out his torch too. They turn them on. The lights dim so that the torch beams can be seen like light sabres. Both Darth Vader and Luke make loud buzzing, sizzling noises.

6 The duel. Darth Vader stays on the stool and turns round on it as Luke dashes about, throws himself across the floor, yells 'Aaagh!' and so on. Keep making buzzing noises as the torch beams clash.

7 Make it look as if Darth Vader has won; Luke falls to his knees and doesn't move. Darth Vader switches off his torch. The lights come on. Then your friend who is operating the tape recorder says in a mysterious voice: 'Luke, this is Obi Wan Kenobi. You are the only one who can save the universe. You can do it, Luke. Just feel the force . . .'

8 Luke says bravely: 'I'll try Obi Wan – I'll try.' The lights go out again and he lunges at Darth Vader with his torch beam. The lights come on again.

9 Darth Vader: 'Aaaagh! Aaaaagh! And more Aaaaagh!' He begins to shrink slowly. Climb down from the stool, fall on your knees and eventually end up flat on your back, pretending to be dead.

10 Luke: 'I've saved the universe! Hooray!' He pulls off the box that hides Darth Vader's face and says 'Daddy!' The lights go out and both of you leave the room as quickly as possible.

WARNING: Because it's difficult to see anything with a cardboard box on your head, the person playing Darth Vader shouldn't attempt to move around too much. Nothing looks more stupid than the most evil person in the universe bumping blindly into a wall! (On the other hand, it will get you a big laugh . . .) Be careful!

THE DUCHESS OF YORK or Fergie!!

A few hundred years ago if anyone did an impersonation of a member of the Royal Family they lost their heads – literally! These days it's not so dangerous, though if you do a very funny impression of Fergie you might blow your chances of ever being awarded a knighthood!

WHAT YOU NEED:
★ A headscarf
★ Any clothes you like (The stranger the mix, the better. A frilly dress and high heels worn under an anorak looks particularly good!)
★ A large handbag
★ A cushion or small pillow
★ A pair of large old-fashioned stereo headphones *or* woolly earmuffs
★ Bunch of flowers
★ Brown eye liner pencil

PUTTING IT TOGETHER:
1 Use the eyeliner to dot your face with freckles.

2 Put on your outfit. The stranger it looks, the better. Stick the cushion down the back of the skirt to give yourself a big bottom.

3 Put on the headscarf and tie it firmly under the chin (unless you have long red hair, in which case forget the scarf). Put the headphones or woolly earmuffs over the top of the scarf.

4 Carry the flowers and handbag.

WHAT YOU DO:

1 Walk into a room. Do a big double-take, as if you're tremendously surprised. Take a step back and with an exaggerated gesture put your right hand over your heart. Lean backwards a few inches. Give a massive grin, opening your eyes wide and boggling as if you can't believe what you're seeing. Straighten up, still smiling, and give a quick wave with your right hand. Say: 'Hi!'

2 Look around the audience. Say: 'How are you? I'm okay, yah!' Take off the headphones. 'I've just flown down from Balmoral.' Grin and boggle your eyes a bit more. 'Andrew has just come back from overseas, you know. He had a very jolly time. Yah, he did. He was flying his plane over a campsite one day when the engine failed. He pressed the ejector button and glided down to earth in his parachute, but unfortu-

nately he landed in a cooking pot. There he was, up to his waist in hot soup and a camper came over and said – you'll never believe this!' Laugh and boggle your eyes. 'The camper said, "What's this flier doing in my soup?"' Laugh, boggle your eyes and look silly.

3 Say: 'It's been lovely seeing you all, but I must fly . . .' and make your exit, waving royally and pulling faces.

GYLES BRANDRETH

Sometimes it seems that whenever you switch on the television set one face always appears – Gyles Brandreth's! In his silly sweaters and amazing hats there's no mistaking him, which makes him an impressionist's dream!

WHAT YOU NEED:
* A sweater with a picture on the front
  or
* A plain round-necked sweater, sheets of paper, coloured pens and safety pins
  or
* An old long-sleeved T-shirt in a pale colour and some felt pens
* A baseball cap
* A small teddy bear or other soft toy
* Safety pins
* Sheets of paper with scribbles on them to look like letters

PUTTING IT TOGETHER:

1 If you don't have a sweater with a picture, draw a suitable picture on a piece of paper, colour it in, cut it out and attach it to the plain jumper with safety pins *or* draw a picture directly onto your *old* T-shirt using felt pens.

2 Take the baseball cap and pin the teddy bear to the top using safety pins. Put on the cap and sweater.

WHAT YOU DO:

1 Study the way that Gyles Brandreth talks. You will notice that he emphasises certain words and rolls his 'R's. Practise doing this. Also practise his expressions, including rolling your eyes and looking surprised.

2 Try telling some silly jokes in his character. You could start with: 'My name is Gyles Brandreth. Yes it is, I promise you!' Lean forward and boggle your eyes. 'Lots of people write to me to find out where I get my jumpers from. Today I'm going to let you into my secret. My dear mother knits them. Oh yes she does!' Peer at the audience again. 'My mother is not only a brilliant knitter, she's also very fast and she knits all the time. Whatever she does she always has a pair of needles in her hand. She was once speeding up the M1 when a police car overtook her and spotted that she was knitting while she was driving! "Pull over!" shouted one of the policemen. "No," yelled my mother. "Socks!"'

BLACK AND WHITE CHARLIE CHAPLIN

Not many people know that Charlie Chaplin's famous tramp costume was flung together in just a few minutes using other people's clothing! He borrowed the trousers from heavyweight comedian Fatty Arbuckle and the hat, moustache and jacket from other friends! The shoes were size 14 and so huge that he had to wear them on the wrong feet to keep them on. The only part of the original outfit that belonged to Chaplin himself was the cane!

WHAT YOU NEED:
★ A pair of baggy black trousers
★ Belt
★ An *old* black jacket that looks a bit small on you
★ Safety pins
★ An *old* white shirt
★ An *old* grey waistcoat
★ A black tie
★ A black bowler hat *or* an old felt hat with a brim you can trim into shape
★ The largest, scruffiest pair of black shoes you can find
★ A garden cane or old walking stick
★ Sandpaper

- ★ Grey poster paint
- ★ Black gloves
- ★ Small piece of black paper
- ★ Blu-tack or spirit gum
- ★ Horror Make-Up (see page 33)

PUTTING IT TOGETHER:

1 Go to local jumble sales and charity shops in your search for the trousers, jacket, waistcoat and hat. With a bit of luck you'll be able to pick up everything you need for just a pound or two. Try the trousers on and turn them up if they are too long. Remember, though, that they are supposed to look huge.

2 Charlie Chaplin wore what was known as a 'cut-away' jacket. You can get the same effect by turning back the front sections of the jacket and safety-pinning them or tacking them up inside.

CHARLIE CHAPLIN'S CUTAWAY-STYLE COAT

THE FRONT FLAPS OF THE JACKET ARE TURNED *INSIDE* THE JACKET AND SAFETY-PINNED IN PLACE.

TWIRLING THE CANE

3 Try the bowler hat on for size. It should look a bit small, so if it's too big crumple up some newspaper and stuff the crown until it sits properly on your head. If you haven't been able to get hold of a bowler, trim the brim of the felt hat into a circular shape. Stuff the crown with newspaper to give it that rounded look.

4 Take the old walking stick or cane, rub it down with the sandpaper and give it a coat or two of grey poster paint.

5 Make up your face in shades of white, black and grey (this is described on page 33) so that you look as if you've just stepped out of a black and white film. Cut out a piece of card measuring 4cm × 2cm. Cut one of the long sides into a slight curve and snip it at intervals to give it a kind of fringe. This is your moustache. Attach it above your top lip using Blu-tack or spirit gum.

6 Put on your outfit, with your shoes on the wrong feet. You should be covered in shades of black, white and grey apart from your hair and eyes!

WHAT YOU DO:

1 Practise Charlie Chaplin's way of walking. Turn your toes out and stand with heels together. Lift your right foot about 5cm bending your knee outwards as you do so, and step forward. Place your right heel a few inches in front of the middle of your left foot, keeping your toes splayed out. Now repeat with the left foot. Walk like this, with your toes sticking out and placing your feet directly in front of each other.

2 When you've got the hang of the Chaplin shuffle, try twirling your cane. Hold the handle loosely, then sweep the stick in a circle (as shown in the diagram). Practise this outside in the garden and don't start doing it near ornaments, furniture, pets or people!

3 Practise Charlie Chaplin's facial expressions. Keeping your head quite still, try to look at something by your side. Lower your eyebrows and mouth and look miserable. Raise them and look happy. Try to avoid smiling and showing your teeth. Hunch your shoulders and trail your cane behind you on the ground when you want to show that you're sad. Stand straight and twirl your cane when you are pleased.

4 Because he was a silent movie star Charlie Chaplin didn't say anything – so you don't have to say anything either! But you do have to perform some slapstick gags. Practise slipping over on an imaginary banana peel and sitting down with a bump. Get up and have a look for the banana peel. You can't see it so you shrug. Take a step – and slip over on it again. Look for

it once more. This time you pretend to find it. Pick it up, holding it at arm's length, and drop it a few feet away. Smile and rub your hands as if you're pleased to have got rid of it. Continue on your way. Then put your hand to your ear as if you heard someone call you, turn round and go back to where you were – and slip over on it again!

If there is a door nearby, go up to it when it is shut and pretend to try to open it. Make it look as if you're pulling really hard on the handle but pretend that it's stuck. The minute you hear someone coming on the other side of the door, walk away, defeated. Look sad. The door will open easily. When it shuts, go through the mime again. This time when the door opens, dash through it and shut it behind you. Wait a few seconds, then knock. Wait a little longer, then knock again. When someone comes to open it, hold the door shut so that *they* can't open it either!

And remember . . .

It doesn't matter if you don't look exactly like Charlie Chaplin. At the height of his fame dozens of actors imitated him in films and the one who looked most like him was, believe it or not, *Japanese*! In fact many of Charlie Chaplin's imitators looked more like him than he did himself, as he discovered when he entered a Charlie Chaplin look-alike contest. He didn't win it. He didn't even come second. The real Charlie Chaplin was awarded *third prize!*

PEGGY FROM *HI-DE-HI*

Of all the characters in *Hi-De-Hi* Peggy is the one who is most fun to imitate!

WHAT YOU NEED:
★ A nylon overall (preferably a size too small for you)
★ A white nylon shower cap *or* bedcap
★ Clumpy shoes
★ Thick-rimmed glasses
★ Bright red lipstick
★ A tea trolley on wheels
★ An assortment of buckets and mops

PUTTING IT TOGETHER:
1 Apply plenty of bright red lipstick and frizz out your hair at the sides.

2 Put on the overall, the shower cap, the glasses and the shoes.

3 Load the tea trolley with buckets and cleaning equipment, then practise wheeling it around.

WHAT YOU DO:
1 Practise Peggy's accent and frantic gestures and manner.

2 Rush into the room pushing your trolley so that when you stop all your buckets and mops fall over. Pull a horrified face as you pick them up and say: 'Oooh err – Miss Cathcart's going to kill me if she finds out!'

3 When you've picked everything up, stand and look exhausted. Wipe the back of your hand across your forehead, then place it over your heart. Look wilted by hunching your shoulders and slightly bending your knees. Keep pulling faces!

4 Say: 'I've had such a morning! We had cat burglars here at Maplins during the night, you know. We're sure they were cat burglars 'cos they took a saucer and a pint of milk from all the chalets!'

5 Say: 'It's not much fun being a chalet maid, you know. I have to put up with all sorts of cheek from people. Just the other day one of the campers said to me, "You've got your cap on back to front." What a nerve! I said, "I wish you'd mind your own business. How do you know which way I'm going?"' Laugh enthusiastically.

6 Say: 'I don't really want to be a chalet maid, you know. I want to be a Yellow Coat!' At this point clutch your hands together under your chin as if you were praying. Say firmly: 'And I *could* be a Yellow Coat. I'm just as good as

Gladys and Spike and the rest of them. Shall I sing you a song?'

7 At this point your audience may yell 'No'. If they do, just say, 'I know you do really,' and launch into your favourite song of the moment. Sing loudly and confidently but *very badly*, with lots of wrong notes. Get the words muddled up, too. If you have the chance, go down on one knee and act very dramatically.

8 Before people start throwing things at you, put your hand to your ear as if you can hear someone coming, and stop singing. Say: 'Ooh-er, I can hear Miss Cathcart coming!' Curtsey quickly, then push the trolley out of the room. Once outside bash the buckets and mops about so that it sounds as if you've had an accident and say loudly, 'I'm ever so sorry, Miss Cath-cart!'

****

GARY'S STAR TIP

If you're doing an impression of an old lady, you may want to give the illusion of having varicose veins. You can do this by taking an old pair of your mother's tights (ask permission first!) and drawing veins on them using a blue felt pen. Then put the tights on!

****

GARY'S STAR TIP

I make my false moustaches myself – and you can make them too. Take some double-sided sticky tape and cut out the rough shape of the moustache. Then use tweezers to stick on some hair clippings (keep yours next time you get your hair cut) or short strands of wool. You can trim the hair or wool into shape, then stick the moustache to your lip. Use this technique for false eyebrows, too.

GARY'S STAR TIP

For a bald wig I use a flesh-coloured swimming cap. If you don't like that idea, you could make a bald head for yourself using a balloon and papier mâché. Blow the balloon up to roughly the size of your head and cover the top part with pieces of newspaper soaked in wallpaper paste. *When the paper has dried out* you can burst the balloon. You'll be left with a shell shape that you can cut carefully to fit your head and paint a flesh colour. Alternatively you could cover the shell with wool or strands of crêpe paper to make yourself a wig.

```
*****************************************
*  GARY'S STAR TIP                      *
*  If you want long, pointed fingernails you *
*  don't have to spend months growing    *
*  them. Cut out cardboard nails, colour them *
*  in with felt pen and stick them on with *
*  sticky tape. Or even better, cut up an old, *
*  clean washing-up liquid container and  *
*  snip some nails from it. You can paint the *
*  white side with paint or nail varnish and *
*  stick them in place by coating your own *
*  nails with clear varnish and pressing the *
*  plastic ones into position while they are *
*  still wet.                             *
*****************************************
```

```
*****************************************
*  GARY'S STAR TIP                      *
*  If you need a pair of glasses to do an *
*  impression of Elton John or Dame Edna *
*  Everage, make your own outrageous specs *
*  using wire, the kind you can buy from  *
*  Do-It-Yourself or electrical shops, and *
*  bending it into the basic shape, with two *
*  arms to go over your ears. Then draw the *
*  shape of the frames on a sheet of firm *
*  cardboard, colour them in, cut them out *
*  carefully and attach them to the wire frame *
*  using glue, sticky tape or more thin pieces *
*  of wire.                               *
*****************************************
```

```
***********************************************
*                                             *
* GARY'S STAR TIP                             *
* To make yourself look as if you've got huge *
* shoulders, pad your jacket with a rolled-up *
* towel across the back of your jacket. For a *
* fat stomach put a small cushion down the    *
* front of your trousers!                     *
*                                             *
***********************************************
```

```
***********************************************
*                                             *
* GARY'S STAR TIP                             *
* For impressions of people with prominent    *
* teeth, like Cilla Black, try making yourself*
* some false teeth using an empty clean       *
* washing-up liquid bottle. Using scissors,   *
* cut it up and snip out a set of suitable white*
* teeth. If you cut a narrow band eight or ten*
* centimetres long attached to the teeth      *
* you'll be able to slip them under your top  *
* lip and keep them in place (see the Count   *
* Dracula Instant Impersonation for a dia-    *
* gram). Personally I think it's even funnier *
* if your teeth keep falling out!             *
*                                             *
***********************************************
```

```
***********************************************
*                                             *
* GARY'S STAR TIP                             *
* If you want to make yourself look really    *
* strange, you can black out a few of your    *
* teeth using tiny pieces of black paper.     *
* Smile please! Oh dear . . .                 *
*                                             *
***********************************************
```

GARY'S STAR TIP

Try padding your cheeks and lips with pieces of cotton wool, clean foam rubber or tissues to see how different you can make yourself look! Just a little bit of padding inside your bottom lip can transform your looks – but be careful not to swallow it!

GARY'S STAR TIP

If the character you are doing an impression of has a limp and you keep forgetting it, put a small stone in your shoe – then you'll limp naturally!

GARY'S STAR TIP

To make a horrible hairy wart, take a small piece of pink Blu-tack-style material and mould it into the right shape, then stick a few hairs from a paintbrush into it. Ugh!

GARY'S STAR TIP

To experiment with your looks, try parting your hair in a different way or combing it all backwards or forwards. You'll be surprised at what a difference it can make to your face.

INSTANT IMPRESSIONS

When you need to do an impression at short notice and there's no time to get a complicated costume organised, try one of these instant impersonations. They're ideal for fancy dress parties and you probably already own nearly all the bits and pieces required!

My favourite instant impression is one I used to do of Hitler playing a penny whistle – it's a bit cheeky. All you need for it is an artist's paint-brush. Place the hairy end of the brush so that it sits up on your top lip like Hitler's little moustache and hold the handle of the brush like a whistle or recorder. Move your fingers up and down as if you're playing it and whistle a tune as you do it!

Napoleon/Nelson

WHAT YOU NEED:

★ A cushion
★ A dark-coloured jacket
★ For Napoleon a sheet of paper, for Nelson a small piece of firm cardboard (the back of a cereal packet is ideal)
★ Coloured felt pens
★ A stapler
★ A safety pin
★ A piece of elastic long enough to go around your head
★ A toy telescope *or* a pair of binoculars (for Nelson only)
★ Trousers
★ Football socks/wellington boots

CUSHION

PUSH ONE CORNER IN WITH YOUR HAND TO MAKE A HOLLOW TRIANGULAR SHAPE.

NAPOLEON

NELSON

WHAT YOU DO:

Napoleon

1 Grab a mug, draw round it on the paper and cut the circle out. Cut two long strips of paper, staple them together, pleat them quickly and staple them around the circle to make a rosette-style medal. If you've got two minutes spare, colour it in very roughly.

2 Put on the trousers and tuck them into the wellington boots.

3 Take the cushion and push one corner inwards, as shown in the diagram. Make a hollow inside the cushion with your hand. Pin the rosette to the front, then put this three-cornered hat on your head with the points facing outwards at the sides.

84

4 Put the jacket on and do the buttons up. Put your right hand under the flap of the jacket as if it was a sling.

5 Stride around saying, 'Not tonight, Josephine' in a French accent.

(*Note:* Depending on the way your jacket does up (left over right or right over left) you may have to cheat and use the wrong arm as the 'dead' one.)

Nelson

1 Make yourself an eye patch by cutting out a 5cm square of paper, rounding off the corners and colouring it black. Attach it to the elastic using staples or by making two small holes, threading the elastic through and tying knots. Put the eye patch on.

2 Put on the trousers, then the socks. Tuck the trousers into the socks.

3 Take the cushion and make the hat in the same way as for Napoleon, above. Put it on with the points facing back and front.

4 Put your left arm into the jacket sleeve and put the jacket on. Keep your right arm by your side. Get someone to help you do the jacket buttons up, still keeping your right arm inside. Now cross the spare right sleeve over the front of the jacket, tuck it inside and use a safety-pin to keep it in place.

5 Stride around saying, 'England expects every man to do his duty' or 'Kiss me, Hardy', whichever you prefer.

Nick Kamen

This impression is strictly for the boys!

WHAT YOU NEED:
- ★ Levi 501 jeans (if you're going to do it properly. Other makes of jeans will do if necessary)
- ★ White football shorts *or* boxer shorts (wear briefs underneath)
- ★ A plain white T-shirt
- ★ White socks
- ★ Deck shoes
- ★ Tape of 'I Heard It Through The Grapevine' and tape recorder to play it on
- ★ Front-loading washing machine

WHAT YOU DO:
1 Put on all the clothes.

2 Turn on the tape recorder and saunter into the kitchen (or wherever you keep the washing machine).

3 Open the washing-machine door (this impression is difficult to carry off successfully if you have a twin tub, but you could try!)

4 Very coolly strip off the T-shirt and throw it into the machine.

5 Bend down and casually take off your shoes and socks and put them in too.

6 Take off your jeans and bundle them in. Shut the washing-machine door, stand up, flex your muscles and coolly saunter out of the kitchen. Wait for everyone to go wild! Strictly speaking, after this impression you should spend the rest of the evening wearing nothing but your shorts.

WARNING: If you're going to do this impression at a party in the winter, check whether there will be central heating available – otherwise you'll freeze!

Ethel from EastEnders

WHAT YOU NEED:
Raid your mother or grandmother's wardrobe – with her permission, of course – and find:

* A crimplene or nylon dress
* A woolly cardigan
* A woolly hat (if you can't find one, try the tea-cosy for size)
* Thick tights or stockings
* Slippers
* A plastic bucket and mop
* A brown eyeliner pencil
* Talcum powder
* A toy dog (if you're absolutely desperate a teddy bear will do)

WHAT YOU DO:
1 Draw plenty of lines on your face with the eyebrow pencil, then dust your face with a little talcum powder.

2 Frizz your hair out and dust it with talc to make it look grey.

3 Put on the dress, cardigan and hat. Climb into the tights or stockings, making sure they're all wrinkly at the ankles. Finish off with the slippers and carry the plastic bucket and mop.

4 Hide the toy dog or teddy somewhere in the house. If it doesn't look anything like Willy, make a notice saying 'Willy' and hang it round its neck. Shuffle round chatting to people about what Albert Square was like in the old days. Then suddenly say in a tremulous voice, "Ere, has anyone seen Willy? I've lost Willy! What am I going to do?' Wail and moan, then organise a massive search for him and insist on kissing the person who eventually finds him!

Coronation Street Variation

By varying this costume slightly you can turn Ethel into Hilda Ogden of *Coronation Street* fame. Add a big apron or a buttoned-up rain-coat, a headscarf and three hair-curlers. Put the apron on over the dress and cardigan, cover your hair completely with the headscarf and tie it neatly at the front. Insert the hair-curlers in your fringe and carry the bucket and mop. Go up to people and say, 'I've got something very important to tell you, chuck,' then tell them an outrageous piece of gossip or a silly story about the Martians landing in the local park.

WARNING: By going to a party as Ethel or Hilda Ogden you will make yourself very popular with the hosts. You can stay behind when everyone else has gone and help with the cleaning and mopping up!

Florence Nightingale

Florence Nightingale was the woman who founded professional nursing as we know it today. She volunteered to work as a nurse during the Crimean War and ran the army hospital wonderfully well, saving many lives. At night, she would walk round the wards carrying an oil lamp and for this reason she became known as the lady with the lamp. As it's a bit unusual to have oil lamps at home these days, try an electric one and make a terrific fancy dress party outfit!

WHAT YOU NEED:

★ A large white apron or a white sheet
★ Red crêpe paper or a sheet of white paper and red pencil or pens
★ A large lampshade (ask your parents if you can borrow one from the light fittings at home)
★ A table lamp or reading lamp

- ★ Safety pins
- ★ A piece of white cardboard measuring approximately 50cm long and 10cm wide
- ★ A stapler
- ★ A first aid kit or an old biscuit tin containing plasters and bandages

WHAT YOU DO:

1 Cut a large red cross from the crêpe paper or make one with your white paper and colour it quickly. Using safety pins, attach it to the front of the apron, or drape the sheet around you, fasten it in place at the shoulder and pin the cross to the front.

2 Fold the cardboard band around your head, trim it if it is too long and staple it so that it sits around your forehead like a crown. If you have

a minute to spare, cut the top so that it is higher at the front than at the back. Draw a big red cross on the front.

3 Put the lampshade on your head and carry the table lamp and the first aid kit.

4 Florence Nightingale was rather a bossy lady, so go up to people and *insist* that they need a plaster or a bandage. Have a terrific time bandaging them up and sticking on plasters.

Barry Manilow

You don't have to love Barry Manilow's music to do this hilarious impression of him! If you're tall, thin and blond you'll find it easy.

WHAT YOU NEED:

★ A V-necked sweater (preferably in a pale colour)
★ Smart shirt and trousers
★ A packet of pink-coloured Blu-tack *or* pink Plasticine
★ Any Barry Manilow record or tape and something to play it on
★ A piano (not absolutely necessary, but it helps)

WHAT YOU DO:

1 Using the pink-coloured Plasticine or Blu-tack material, build yourself a false nose. It's useful to model it on one of your fingers (see the diagram) because then it will be the right shape to attach to your nose.

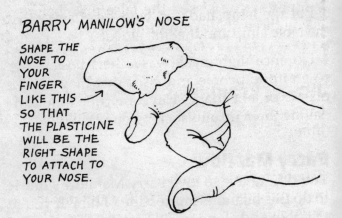

BARRY MANILOW'S NOSE

SHAPE THE NOSE TO YOUR FINGER LIKE THIS → SO THAT THE PLASTICINE WILL BE THE RIGHT SHAPE TO ATTACH TO YOUR NOSE.

2 Put on the shirt, trousers and sweater.

3 Practise Barry Manilow's gestures and movements. These will depend a lot on the song you have chosen. Work them out for yourself, but remember to smile a lot and be sincere.

4 Apply your false nose.

5 If there's a piano, sit at it. If not, mime piano-playing. Turn on the record or tape and try to get through a whole song before your nose drops off. When the song finishes stand up, say 'I love you all,' bow, pull off your nose (if it hasn't already fallen off), throw it into the audience and make your triumphant exit.

```
************************************************
*                                              *
* GARY'S STAR TIP                              *
* I think this impression would be even more   *
* funny if you kissed the false nose before    *
* you threw it into the audience!              *
*                                              *
************************************************
```

Jimmy Krankie

Girls *and* boys can have a go at imitating wee Jimmy!

WHAT YOU NEED:
School uniform, ideally:

★ A red cap
★ A blue shirt
★ A navy school blazer
★ Grey shorts
★ Grey socks
★ Lace-up shoes
★ A school tie

★ A water pistol
★ A plastic spider
★ A plastic banana and any other practical joke equipment you can lay hands on

WHAT YOU DO:

1 Put on the school uniform.

2 Run into the room. Yell 'Fandabidozi!'. Do a thumbs up sign using both thumbs. Run round getting in people's way and saying sorry, then pulling a face as if you don't really mean it.

3 Turn to the nearest person and say 'Hey, Mister' (or 'Hey, Missus') in a strong Scottish

accent. When he (or she) turns round, squirt them in the face with the water pistol. Double up with laughter and keep laughing, whatever they do.

4 Keep playing silly practical jokes on people – putting a plastic spider down the back of their neck, for example, or offering them a plastic banana to eat. Avoid any jokes that create a mess or could damage people or furnishings in any way.

5 Make a general nuisance of yourself, saying silly things, telling terrible jokes.

WARNING: Do not take this impersonation too far. If you make yourself too much of a pest you might be thrown out!

Clint and Clyde

Here's another Clint Eastwood impression, but this time you don't have to dress up quite so much. This is the Clint who starred in *Every Which Way But Loose* with his friend Clyde the orang-utan!

WHAT YOU NEED:
★ Jeans
★ Shirt
★ Brown eye pencil
★ Large toy monkey (or a real-live orang-utan if you happen to have one around the house)
★ Safety pins

WHAT YOU DO:

1 Using the eybrow pencil, dot your chin and cheeks so that you look as if you have a stubbly beard. Rub in gently with your fingertips.

2 Put on jeans and shirt.

3 Take the toy monkey and attach it to your shoulders or round your neck using safety pins.

4 Practise the art of narrowing your eyes so that you can barely see out of them and giving people a good hard stare. Wander around looking mean and moody. If anyone does anything to catch your attention – such as get in your way, drop something, giggle loudly – stare at them and grunt, 'Wanna make my day, punk?'

All-Purpose National Leader Outfit

All the best known national leaders these days seem to be women and you can use this all-purpose outfit to impersonate most of them – including Mrs Thatcher and the Queen.

WHAT YOU NEED:

★ A twinset and pearls
★ A smart skirt
★ A wig or a headscarf
★ A large handbag
★ Talcum powder
★ Pink blusher
★ For the Queen, a plastic sword (or, in the last resort, a broom handle)

WHAT YOU DO:

1 Apply a dab of pink blusher to each cheek, dust your face liberally with talcum powder, put on the twinset and pearls and top the lot off with either the wig or the headscarf. If you don't want to use these, and if you've got shortish hair, have it set with rollers to give you a middle-aged look. Perhaps your mother has some heated hair-rollers and will help you?

2 Slip your arm through the handbag strap and clutch it firmly in the crook of your elbow. The bigger and more bulky the handbag, the better.

For Mrs Thatcher

1 Watch *Spitting Image* and practise Mrs Thatcher's very distinctive accent.

2 Be bossy. Go up to people, interrupt them, grab their hands and shake them firmly and for a long time. Say 'How do you do? I'm Margaret Thatcher. I hope you voted for me in the last election.' If they say they did, pat them warmly on the back and say, 'Jolly good. What a clever fellow you are.' If they say they didn't, say, 'Never mind, everyone else did,' or cry 'What???' and hit them (gently!) with your handbag.

3 If there's a sideboard, a kitchen cupboard or something similar in the room, go up to someone and say, 'I wonder if you would like to be in my cabinet?' If they say yes, show them to the cupboard, open the door and tell them in a bossy voice, 'Well, get in then!'

For the Queen
1 Watch *Spitting Image* and practise the Queen's accent.

2 Enter the room, raise your right hand and move it from side to side about 15cm to give a royal wave. The Queen does **not** wave like ordinary people.

3 Whatever happens, *never* smile. Try to look bored. Go round the room shaking hands with everyone (hold their hands very limply) and say-things like, 'Nice weather we're having . . .' and 'Do you like corgis?'

4 When you get tired of this and you've shaken hands with everyone in the room, ask a flunky (that's an assistant) to fetch your sword (or broom handle) and knight a few people.

Sir Robin Day
The most important thing about this impression is the voice. When you say anything, try to make it sound as if you have just run a kilometre or two.

WHAT YOU NEED:
★ A suit
★ A bow tie
★ Thick-rimmed glasses

WHAT YOU DO:

1 Walk in and wheeze a little.

2 Point to someone. Say loudly: 'That gentle-man (or lady) over there. I believe you wanted to say something?'

3 If they insist that they *don't* have anything to say, snap angrily, and say 'Well in that case I wish you wouldn't keep putting your hand up.'

4 Turn to someone else. Wheeze and gurgle a bit. Say, 'Come on, come on, we don't have all day you know! What do *you* think about the growing menace of Postman Pat? Should cats be allowed to ride in Post Office vans?' (Or insert the silliest question you can think of.)

5 Keep asking questions and jumping from person to person. After a few minutes say, 'Well, we've got to end it there I'm afraid. Goodnight to you all – and especially to *you*,' and make your exit.

Instant Count Dracula

WHAT YOU NEED:
- ★ An orange
- ★ A black cloak or blanket
- ★ Hair gel or water
- ★ Talcum powder

WHAT YOU DO:

1 Peel the orange carefully, trying to keep it in one large piece. Cut a piece of peel about 7cm

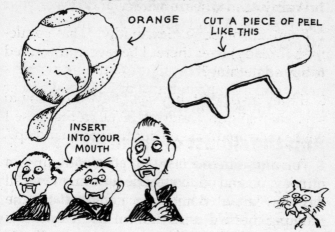

COUNT DRACULA'S TEETH

ORANGE

CUT A PIECE OF PEEL LIKE THIS

INSERT INTO YOUR MOUTH

long and 3cm deep. Cut this as shown in the diagram, and make yourself a set of fangs. Insert between your top lip and teeth, with the pith side showing. Practise covering your fangs with your lower lip, then smiling and revealing them!

2 Give your face a good coating of talcum powder so that you look deathly pale.

3 Using hair gel or water, comb all your hair backwards off your face and slick it down.

4 Wrap the black cloak or blanket around you so that when you hold your arms outstretched at your side it flaps out like a bat's wings.

5 Walk up to people with your fangs hidden. Keeping your lips almost closed, say: 'Do you

99

know what my favourite song is?' They will probably say no. Grin widely and reveal your vampire teeth and say: 'It's "Fangs for the Memory"!'

6 Spend the rest of the time examining people's necks and asking your host or hostess whether there's any garlic in the sandwiches.

And the silliest of them all . . .

If you and a friend need an absolutely instant impression and you've got no time to prepare at all, how about doing this impersonation of Phillip Schofield and Gordon the Gopher of Children's BBC fame?

WHAT YOU NEED:
★ A sofa or some other piece of solid furniture with a high back
★ Two people

WHAT YOU DO:

1 Turn the sofa so that the back of it is facing the audience.

2 The person who is imitating Phillip Schofield should kneel on the seat of the sofa and lean his arms on the top.

3 The person playing Gordon rolls up his right sleeve and crouches down on the sofa seat on the left-hand side of 'Phillip'.

4 'Phillip' says brightly: 'Hello again! This is Children's BBC, I'm Phillip Schofield and . . .'

5 At this point 'Gordon' sticks his right hand and wrist up above the sofa. Hold the four fingers of your hand together. Bend them so that your forefinger touches the tip of your thumb (see the diagram). Open and shut your hand a couple of times as if Gordon is speaking, making squeaking noises as you do so. Move your hand backwards and forwards along the back of the sofa as if he is running up and down.

6 'Phillip' looks at this sight and goes 'Aaaagh!' Look shocked and stunned and then says loudly, 'And this is Gordon – and he's got no clothes on!!'

CRAZY IMPRESSIONS

What should you do if you have no talent for copying other people's accents, you hate having to get dressed up in a costume, you're too lazy to do anything energetic but you *still* want to do an impression for your friends or at a party? You should do a completely crazy impression, that's what. I used to think some of my own impressions were pretty crazy, but wait until you've seen these!

1 Lie flat on the floor until someone notices you. If they ask what you are tell them to pull your feet while someone else pulls your arms. When they both pull hard, shout, 'Bang!!' as loudly as you can and reveal that you *were* a Christmas cracker.

2 Curl up on a chair and pretend to be fast asleep. If anyone wants to know who you are tell them that you're Postman Pat's cat Jess, you've had a busy morning out in Postman Pat's van and all you want is a chance to snooze.

3 Walk around smiling at no one in particular. Pick things up, put them down, smile vaguely and walk out again. Turn to someone and say something to them, but instead of making a noise just move your lips. If anyone asks what you've come as tell them you're an extra from *Crossroads*. (The *Crossroads* extras are those actors who walk around the motel saying nothing and pretending to be guests.)

4 Put a yellow pillowcase or towel over your head and sit absolutely still. If you have to move, make a slurping noise. What are you? A bowl of custard, of course . . .

5 Stand or lie silently in a corner. Keep absolutely still with your eyes shut. If people ask who you've come as, say you're the robot 'C3PO' from *Star Wars*. Explain that you are in disguise because you are on a mission to save the Earth but that you're suffering from a computer malfunction. When you're bored with this you can walk around stiffly and tell everyone that you've been mended.

6 Put a very small sprig of holly in your hair or pocket. If asked, tell people that they are not going to believe it but you're Santa Claus. Explain that you're out of uniform because it's not yet Christmas. If they say they don't believe you, threaten not to deliver their Christmas presents this year!

7 Walk around with your back bent. Keep swishing your bottom as if you had a tail attached. Tell people that you're the back half of a pantomime horse and ask if they've seen the front half. (Don't do this impression if you suffer from back trouble . . .)

8 Lie silently flat on your back with your eyes closed. If anyone asks, tell them you are Queen Victoria or William Shakespeare, or anyone else who has been dead for a long time.

9 Crawl around the house on your hands and knees dragging a toilet roll behind you with one end in your teeth. You are, of course, doing an excellent impression of the Andrex puppy. (WARNING: Do not use the last toilet roll in the bathroom and make sure you clear up *all* the mess afterwards!)

10 Lie in a chair or sofa and pretend to be asleep. When anyone asks, explain that you are doing an impression of a BBC newsreader (or weatherman if you prefer) between news (or weather) bulletins.

JOKE FILE

People are always asking me where I find all the jokes and material for my act. I'll let you into a secret: I get quite a lot of them from ordinary people who like to tell me their latest joke when they see me at motorway service stations and places like that!

Sometimes, I start with a character and look for jokes for him or her to tell, but more often than that I hear a really good joke and I think to myself, 'If Kenneth Williams or Norman Wisdom told that joke it would be even more funny' – and so I do an impression of them.

In this section you'll find lots of funnies. Some of them are Star Jokes, for which I've suggested a character who might tell the jokes to make them even more amusing.

★ GARY'S STAR JOKES ★

Try telling this joke as Alexis from *Dynasty*. If you're wearing a fur coat it would be even funnier.

Why do cats wear fur coats?

Because they look silly in plastic macs!

Doctor, doctor, I feel like a snooker ball!
Go to the end of the queue (cue).

What is Count Dracula's favourite sport?
Batminton.

ALEXIS: Have you ever seen me on television?
VIEWER: Yes, on and off.
ALEXIS: And how do you like me?
VIEWER: Off.

What happened when the idiot jumped into the Thames?
He got wet.

★ GARY'S STAR JOKES ★

I think Jimmy Cricket would be best to tell this joke:

A man went to buy some invisible ink in Ireland. 'Certainly, sir,' said the shop assistant. 'What colour?'

★ GARY'S STAR JOKES ★

Try telling these three jokes while you're doing an impression of Clint Eastwood:

Where do cowboys keep their water?
In their ten-gallon hats.

Why do cowboys die with their boots on?
So they don't stub their toes when they kick the bucket.

What's made of sugar and swings through the trees in the jungle?
A meringue-utan.

★ GARY'S STAR JOKES ★

I thought this would be funny for Madonna and Darth Vader:
MADONNA: What does it feel like to hurtle through space?
DARTH VADER: It hurtles!

What do you call a madman in space?
An astronut.

What song does the most conceited singer in the world love best?
'The Best Things in Life Are Me.'

Why can't Jimmy Krankie sleep in class?
Because the teacher talks too loudly!

★ GARY'S STAR JOKES ★

How about telling this joke as Peggy from
Hi-De-Hi?
'Doctor, doctor, I've just swallowed a roll
of film!'
'Let's hope nothing develops.'

When is it a good idea for Clint Eastwood to lose
his temper?
When he's in a bad one . . .

Who was the most popular actor in the Bible?
Samson – he brought the house down!

★ GARY'S STAR JOKES ★

News jokes are always fun. An impression of Sir Robin Day reading these crazy news flashes would be funny, but I think Norman Wisdom would be even better:

'Here is the news: Thousands of mattresses have been stolen from a local factory. Police are reported to be springing into action . . . News has just come in that the marriage of two lighthouse keepers in Scotland is on the rocks . . . A burglar caught stealing a camping stove last Thursday has been charged with robbery within tent . . . Station staff at Charing Cross have apologised for the fact that all the trains were ten minutes late today. Tomorrow they will be back to normal – fifteen minutes late . . . And we have just heard that the last white-tailed African antelope in the world has been shot. So that is the end of the gnus . . .'.

Jimmy Krankie's teacher was handing back the homework assignments that she had just marked. 'Did your brother help you with your science questions?' she asked. 'No, Miss,' said Jimmy. 'I got them wrong all by myself!'

If you can do an impression of Keith Harris and Orville, you might like to try this joke:
What happens to a duck before it grows up?
It grows down.

What's orange and comes out of the ground at 200 k.p.h.?
A jet-propelled carrot!

Here's another joke that would be ideal for Jimmy Krankie to tell about himself:
'Do you know what happened when I swallowed some uranium in the science lesson the other day? I got atomic ache.'

110

Try telling this joke in the style of Kenneth
Williams *and* Jimmy Cricket:
KENNETH: I went to a restaurant where
they'd thrown away all the menus.
JIMMY: How did you know what to order?
KENNETH: I looked at the tablecloth and
guessed.

Why is a newspaper like an army?
Because it is full of leaders and columns.

As this is an American joke I think it would
be appropriate for Ronald Reagan to tell it:
Why does the Statue of Liberty stand in
New York habour?
Because she can't sit down.

Here's an ideal joke for Jimmy Krankie and
Jimmy Cricket:
JIMMY CRICKET: Did you hear about the
fight on the train?
JIMMY KRANKIE: What happened?
JIMMY CRICKET: The guard punched a
ticket.

What would happen if you swallowed a frog?
You might croak.

★ GARY'S STAR JOKES ★

A joke like this one can be told by almost
anyone. As it's so silly, why not do an
impression of the Queen or Margaret
Thatcher telling it?
Q: What language do twins in Amsterdam
speak?
A: Double Dutch.

What kind of tree does Gyles Brandreth carry
around with him?
A palm.

What happens when you put Alexis and Clint Eastwood together? This is what you get:

ALEXIS: Is it true that if you carry an umbrella a lion won't be able to catch you?

CLINT EASTWOOD: It depends how fast you run while you're carrying it.

FIRST IDIOT: This match won't light.
SECOND IDIOT: It did a minute ago when I tried it!

Here's another joke for the Krankies:

IAN: When you went to Rome did you have any problems with your Italian?

JIMMY KRANKIE: No, but the Italians did!

And here's another crazy combination – Alexis and Jimmy Cricket!

JIMMY CRICKET: How much a pound do people pay for babies?

ALEXIS: People don't buy babies by the pound!

JIMMY CRICKET: So why do they weigh them the minute they're born?

TEACHER: Are you good at arithmetic?
JIMMY KRANKIE: Yes and no.
TEACHER: What do you mean?
JIMMY: Yes, I'm no good at arithmetic.

★ GARY'S STAR JOKES ★

I think this joke is much more funny if you
do it with an impression of the Duchess of
York:
FERGIE: Have you ever seen a Duchess
before?
ADRIAN MOLE: Aren't they the same as
English 'S's?

★ GARY'S STAR JOKES ★

You can use *any* characters for this joke but
I thought Jimmy Cricket and Sir Robin
made a funny combination:
JIMMY CRICKET: I bet I can tell the name
of your wife.
SIR ROBIN DAY: I bet you can't!
JIMMY CRICKET: Yes I can – Mrs Day!

What profession was Noah?
He was an arkitect.

How would you prevent yourself from starving
on a desert island?
By eating the sand-which is there . . .

'Have you heard the joke about the blunt pencil? You wouldn't get the point.'

★ GARY'S STAR JOKES ★

This one *has* to be a joke for Jimmy Cricket because he wears wellies all the time!
Why does Jimmy Cricket keep a dictionary in his wellies?
Because he wants to be a smarty-boots.

Where do gnomes do their shopping?
At British Gnome Stores.

Q: What's brown and yellow and white and travels faster than the speed of sound?
A: A Concorde pilot's egg sandwich.

A man staggered into the Casualty department of a hospital with his clothes ripped and blood streaming from his arm. 'Have an accident?' asked the nurse.

'No thanks,' he moaned. 'I've just had one.'

★ GARY'S STAR JOKES ★

What about Madonna and Clint Eastwood?
MADONNA: Have you ever hunted bear?
CLINT EASTWOOD: No, I always wear my jeans.

What did the lion say when it saw two tourists in a jeep?
'Oh look, meals on wheels . . .'

★ GARY'S STAR JOKES ★

This joke might get a big laugh if you used it for your impression of the Queen:

What is the difference between the Prince of Wales and a tennis ball?

One is heir to the throne and the other is thrown to the air.

PATIENT: Doctor, doctor, I think I'm a dog!
DOCTOR: Sit down please.
PATIENT: I can't – I'm not allowed on the furniture.

Have you heard the story of the three wells?
No.
Well, well, well . . .

What should you do if you swallow a pen?
Use a pencil . . .

★ GARY'S STAR JOKES ★

Here's another joke ideal for Jimmy
Cricket:
JIMMY CRICKET: Hey, Mr Postman, do
you have any letters for me?
POSTMAN: What's your name?
JIMMY CRICKET: It's on the envelope!

Jimmy Cricket has a friend who does bird impressions. He eats worms . . .

Did you hear about the woman who won a
saucepan playing bingo?
It was pot luck.

★ GARY'S STAR JOKES ★

Jimmy Krankie is *always* being rude, so I
thought this joke would suit him.
JIMMY KRANKIE: How old are you:
ALEXIS: Pushing thirty.
JIMMY: Yes, but from which direction?

'I throw myself into everything I do.'
'Why not go and dig a hole then?'

★ GARY'S STAR JOKES ★

How about telling this joke for your impression of Peggy from *Hi-De-Hi*?

Three elderly and rather deaf ladies were sitting together on a park bench. 'It's windy today,' said the first.

'No, it's Thursday,' said the second.

'Yes, I could drink a cup of tea too,' said the third.

★ GARY'S STAR JOKES ★

Here's a final joke that's perfect for your impression of the Krankies:

IAN KRANKIE: Jimmy, you always want your own way.

JIMMY: Well if it's mine, why won't you let me have it?

STORY FILE

If you want to do a longer impression of one of your favourite stars, or perhaps even write your own comedy act, you'll need to tell some funny stories. And to make it easier for you to do that, here's a collection of longer jokes.

It helps if you can be really quick-witted when telling these stories and add things as you go along. A few years ago, I was doing my act in a club in Avonmouth. It was a very small place and always very smoky, but for some reason the smoke seemed much thicker and more choking than usual. Halfway through the act, I noticed a blue light flashing outside and then there was a knock on the emergency fire doors at the side of the stage! As I was nearest to them, I walked over and pushed the doors open – and there were five firemen who'd come to see if the club had been affected by a fire in the place next door. All the smoke had been seeping through air vents, which was why it had been so smoky in the club!

I took the microphone out to the back and started interviewing the firemen and making up jokes as I went along. As you can imagine, by the time I got back into my act, anything I said about fires or smoke had the audience cheering, so I sang 'Smoke Gets in Your Eyes' and told as many jokes about firemen and bonfires as I could think of. I finished off the act with the line, 'When I go to see my agent tomorrow he'll say to me, "How did it go last night, Gary?" and I'll say, '"To be honest, it went down like a house on fire".' It must have made the right impression on the audience because when I went back there the next year I'd just got into my act when there was a knock on the same doors. I opened them, and there were five firemen! It turned out that they were members of the club and had borrowed the uniforms and equipment from the local fire station!

That story just goes to show that although you can prepare all your material in advance, you have to be ready to change it to suit the occasion. You've also got to adapt the story to fit the character you want to tell it. For example, here's a joke that you could use for several impressions, among them Peggy, the chalet maid from *Hi-De-Hi*. Here it is in its *un*adapted form:

A girl met one of her friends, who she hadn't seen for ages, in the street. 'How's your mum and dad?' she asked.

'Didn't you hear?' said the friend. 'My Dad died.'

'That's terrible. How did he die?'

'He went down the garden to pull some

carrots for lunch and collapsed.'

'What did your mum do?' asked the girl.

'Fortunately she had a packet of frozen peas . . .'

And here's how you can adapt it to suit Peggy, taking into account the way she speaks:

'I was out doing some shopping the other day when I bumped into one of the girls who used to work as a chalet maid here at Maplins. We had a lovely chat and I asked her how her old mum and dad were.

"Didn't you hear?" she said. "My Dad died."

Well, you can imagine how I felt, putting my foot in it like that! "Ooh err," I said. "How did your poor dad die?"

"Well," she said. "It was really strange. He went down the garden to pull some carrots for dinner and the next thing he'd collapsed."

"That's terrible," I said. "How did your Mum cope?"

She looked at me and said, "Well, it was lucky really because she had a packet of frozen peas in the fridge."'

Here's a story that you could adapt for a character who is always getting things wrong – like Norman Wisdom or Jimmy Cricket:

A man picked up the telephone and dialled the

operator. 'Can I have the Interpol number, please?'

'You'll have to dial the international operator.' So the man dialled the international operator.

'Get me Interpol please,' he said.

'You'll have to call French Directory Enquiries,' said the operator.

So the man dialled French Directory Inquiries. 'I'd like the number for Interpol, please,' he said.

'It's Paris 76543,' said the operator.

The man dialled the number. ''Allo,' said a French voice. 'Zis is Interpol.'

'Thank goodness,' said the man. 'I'd like to send a large bunch of flowers to my mother . . .'

And there's more . . .

A mother found her young daughter crying miserably on her bed. 'What's wrong?' she enquired anxiously.

'I've just had a letter from my boyfriend,' sobbed the girl, 'and he's put only two kisses at the bottom.'

'Surely that's enough?'

'No, I hate being double-crossed.'

'How many times have I told you that you must wear your school uniform?' yelled a furious teacher to a pupil who had turned up in jeans.

'Go home and change into your school clothes.'

Half an hour later the pupil returned – wearing uniform but soaked from head to foot. 'Why are you wet?' asked the teacher.

'You told me to wear my school clothes,' explained the boy, 'but they were in the wash.'

Have you noticed how expensive fruit can be? A man walked into a lovely greengrocer's shop which was full of exotic fruit and vegetables. But he was stunned when he bought two apples and was charged more than £1. He paid the girl and left the shop clutching his fruit. 'Excuse me,' said the girl, racing after him. 'But you've forgotten your twenty pence change.'

'Keep it,' said the customer. 'I trod on a grape as I came in.'

A boy was telling his best friend how bad his mother's cooking was.

'Last night,' he said, 'she made us soup. It was so disgusting that when we came down to the kitchen this morning we found it full of South American indians who'd come all the way to dip the tips of their arrows into it.'

The Warner family were very worried. They had just heard the news that Granny Warner had won a million pounds on the football pools and they were terrified that if they broke the news to her too quickly the shock would be too much for her poor old heart to stand. Eventually they decided to call the doctor.

'You were very wise to consult me,' he said. 'The news could be too much for her. I'll go and have a chat with her and lead up to it gradually.' The family accepted his offer and that afternoon he arrived to see Granny. After a few minutes of general chat the doctor worked his way round to the subject.

'Tell me, Mrs Warner, what would you do if you suddenly came into a million pounds?'

Granny Warner thought about it for a minute. 'You've always been good to me, doctor, so I'd give half of it to you,' she said at last – and the doctor immediately collapsed and died of shock!

The Smith family had a wonderful holiday on a farm in Devon last summer, and wanted to go back again this year. However, there was one thing they hadn't enjoyed and that was the terrible smell of the pigs which were kept on the farm. Mrs Smith wrote to the farmer to find out whether the pigs were still there. A few days later the reply arrived.

'Don't worry,' it read. 'We haven't had pigs since you were with us last year.'

One fine morning there came a knock on Mrs Brown's front door. She opened it to find a total stranger standing there. 'What can I do for you?' she enquired.

'Forgive me for calling on you,' said the stranger, 'but each morning at 8.30 I pass this house and see you hitting your son over the head with a sliced white loaf.'

'That's right,' said Mrs Brown.

'But yesterday morning I came by and you were hitting him with a strawberry gateau. Have you run out of bread?'

'No,' said Mrs Brown. 'You see, today is his birthday.'

At a country fair, a pilot was selling flights in the open cockpit of his biplane. One elderly couple watched him taking off and landing with various passengers but couldn't decide whether they could afford to go for the ride or not. 'I'll tell you what,' said the pilot. 'If you're good passengers and don't make any noise, I'll take you up for free.'

The couple climbed in and a few seconds later they taxied down the runway and took off. As a special treat, the pilot threw in a few tricks, like looping the loop and flying upside down. Half an hour later when they landed, the pilot congratulated the old gentleman on how quiet he'd been.

'It wasn't easy,' replied the man. 'I nearly yelled when my wife fell out.'

A man went to the fairground and decided he'd try his luck on the darts stall. With his first dart he scored a bullseye and the stall owner handed him his prize – a tortoise. The man was very pleased and went off, carrying his prize. Ten minutes later he came back and had another go, and this time he scored two bullseyes. 'What would you like for your prize this time?' asked the stallholder.

'Oh,' said the man, 'I'll have another of those nice crusty meat pies.'

A family of tortoises, a father, a mother and a baby, went to a pizza parlour for a meal. They all ordered cheese and tomato pizzas but while they were waiting for them to arrive they noticed that it had begun to rain outside. 'Would you nip home and get our umbrellas for us?' the mother tortoise asked the baby tortoise. The baby tortoise wasn't very happy about this because he thought his parents might finish off his pizza while he was gone, but they promised not to so off he went.

The other two tortoises sat in the pizza parlour for the rest of the day. Night came, then dawn, and still they sat there. The days passed. After a week the father tortoise said, 'We might as well eat Junior's pizza.'

'Hey!' came Junior's cry from somewhere near the door. 'If you eat my pizza I won't go for your umbrellas!'

A mean man took his whole family out for a meal in a restaurant. It was a very large meal and they were unable to eat it all. The man beckoned the waiter over to the table and asked whether they could have a plastic bag to take home the leftovers for the dog.

'Gosh,' said his young son, 'does this mean we are going to get a dog, Dad?'

A young country couple went to their local town to visit the fair and decided to try the Tunnel of Love for the first time. When they got home the boy's father asked if he'd enjoyed it.

'No I didn't,' he said. 'It was dark and cold and frightening and we both got soaked to the skin.'

'What happened? Did your boat have a leak?' asked the father.

'There was a boat . . .?'

Two creatures from outer space landed in a small town at four o'clock in the morning. Nearby there was a traffic light. 'I'm going to marry that Earthling,' said the first spaceman.

'I saw her first!' said the other.

'Maybe, but it was me she winked her green eye at.'

A fat lady went into a café, looked at the menu and said to the waiter, 'I'll have a large ice-cream sundae with an extra scoop of strawberry ice, two chocolate flakes and plenty of hot fudge sauce, please.'

The waiter wrote it down. 'And would you like a cherry on the top?'

'No thank you,' said the lady. 'I'm on a diet.'

An American couple called Mr and Mrs Parker were on holiday in Moscow and were shown around by a Russian guide called Rudolph. Mr Parker didn't get on at all well with Rudolph and they spent much of their time arguing. On the last day Rudolph escorted them to the airport and as they drove there Mr Parker said: 'Look, Mildred! It's snowing.'

'It is not snowing,' said Rudolph. 'That is Russian rain.'

'It's snow!' insisted Mr Parker.

'Now, now,' said Mrs Parker to her husband. 'Rudolph the Red knows rain, dear.'

A young man got a job selling encyclopaedias from door to door. On his first day, he knocked on hundreds of doors but didn't manage to sell a single book. Very depressed, he decided to make one last call. He knocked at the door and when a lady answered he launched into his sales pitch, explaining to her that his encyclopaedia was an indispensable collection of human knowledge, a mine of information on every subject she could imagine, including animals, plants, birds, history, geography, physics, chemistry in twelve volumes each containing 1,000 pages and about five centimetres thick . . .

'Hold on just a moment,' said the woman. She went indoors, then came back and said, 'I'll take two volumes.'

'Why only two?' asked the young man. 'It would be better to have all twelve.'

'Because our broken table leg is only ten centimetres short.'

One night out on the range some cowboys were sitting around their camp fire telling stories. One of them said, 'I know an old Indian chief who never forgets anything you say to him. The Devil can take my soul if I'm not telling the truth.'

That night the Devil appeared. 'I was listening last night and I'm here to take your soul if you were lying about that Indian. Take me to him.' So the two of them went to visit the Indian chief.

The Devil asked one simple question. 'Do you like eggs?'

'Yes,' replied the Indian.

The the Devil and the cowboy went their different ways. Some fifteen years later the Devil heard that the cowboy had died. This was his chance to claim his soul, he thought, so he went to see the Indian again. 'How!' he said, greeting the old man.

'Poached,' said the Indian.

Father Bear, Mother Bear and Baby Bear all came in from their morning stroll in the forest. Father Bear looked down at his bowl sitting empty on the table. 'Who's been eating my porridge?' he growled.

Baby Bear looked at his empty bowl sitting on the table. 'And who's been eating my porridge?'

'Shut up you two,' said Mother Bear. 'I haven't had time to make it yet.'

It was lunchtime on the building site and all the workmen were tucking into their sandwiches. 'Oh no,' said one of them as he opened his lunchbox. 'Fish paste. I don't like fish paste.'

He picked up the next sandwich. 'More fish paste. Yuck!' Then he took out all his sandwiches and checked the filling. 'They're *all* fish paste!' he moaned.

'Why don't you tell your wife not to pack you fish paste sandwiches?' asked one of the other builders.

'That wouldn't help,' sighed the man. 'She doesn't make my sandwiches – I do.'

An American man decided he was going to make some money by getting himself knocked down by a bus so that he could claim insurance compensation. He stood at the bus stop and stuck his foot in the road. A few minutes later a bus drove up and ran over his leg. He was in hospital for six weeks but he received $100,000! As soon as he came out of hospital he went to Germany and did the same thing there, receiving 200,000 Deutschmarks for his injuries. In Paris he was awarded 500,000 Francs after being run over by yet another bus! But when he came to London and stood at a bus stop with his leg stuck out into the road, the trick didn't work – he died of pneumonia.

A farmer was chatting to a boy who had come for a holiday on the farm. 'How many cows do you think I've got in this field?' asked the farmer.

The boy looked around for a few seconds, then said, 'Ninety-three.'

'That's incredible,' said the farmer. 'How did you count them so quickly?'

'Well,' said the boy, 'I just counted up the legs and then divided by four.'

HAVE A PARTY!

Wherever I go people are always stopping me and asking me to do a quick impression for them. The problem is, I've never been very good at doing them to order like that. Even when I was just mucking about with friends at school I couldn't do it. But one place you might see me doing impressions – apart from on the stage or TV – is at a party with my friends. It's easier to do impressions when you're enjoying yourself and I always find that if I start doing mine, lots of other people start doing their favourites too, and we end up having a wonderful time.

That gave me an idea. If you love doing impressions and you have friends who do them too, why not hold a party and invite your guests to come as someone else? Not just an ordinary fancy dress party, you understand, but a party where everyone has to do an impression of someone else all the time – while you play games, eat your tea and talk to other people. I think it would be really funny!

Or if you think that is asking too much of your friends, allow them to be themselves for most of the time but ask each of them to do a two-minute impression. You could organise it as if it was a talent show and offer a prize for the person who does the best voice impression, a prize for the best costume and a prize for the funniest impersonation.

You could also organise crazy games which your guests have to play in character. Even the most ordinary party game is hilariously funny if everyone has to pretend to be someone else while they play it. I think some of these could be an absolute riot:

Musical Chairs

Everyone knows how to play that old party-time favourite Musical Chairs. Count up the number of players and put out one fewer chairs. Turn the music on. Everyone walks around the chairs and as soon as the music stops they sit down. The person left standing is out of the game.

Now this may not sound particularly crazy, but imagine playing it with everyone impersonating a character! You could have Clint Eastwood walking around very slowly and threateningly; Jimmy Cricket doing everything wrong; Peggy from *Hi De Hi* pushing her trolley and Norman Wisdom bumping into people, not to mention Darth Vader, Luke Skywalker and Mrs Thatcher all scrambling for seats. *Now that's fun!*

The Picture Frame Game

For this game you need a picture frame without a picture on it. If you can't find one, make a large oblong-shaped frame from cardboard. Take it in turns to hold the frame up around your face and pose like one of those old-fashioned portraits that you see in museums! Whatever happens the person in the picture frame must *not* smile – not even when everyone else does their impression and tells a silly joke. The impressionist who makes the person in the picture laugh wins a point and then it's some-one else's turn to take over!

Three-Legged Race

If you have a big enough garden how about organising a three-legged race, an egg-and-spoon race or even a sack race? The three-legged race is particularly funny because you can put unlikely pairs together. Imagine teaming someone playing Ethel from *EastEnders* with Jimmy Krankie or putting Alexis from *Dynasty* with Charlie Chaplin! Everyone has to run in character – and fall over in character, too!

Nutty Noises

You can play this with one or more of your friends. All you have to do is take turns to think up some extremely unlikely noises and then everyone has to try to imitate them! The one whose impression is judged to be best by the person who nominated the noise scores a point. For example, you could try asking your friends to imitate:

A bowl of custard travelling down the M1 at 120 m.p.h.

A sockful of jelly being thrown by an Australian and hitting a cow.

A runaway bus full of donkeys driving into the sea and hitting the side of the QE II.

Animal Consequences

You don't have to hold a party to enjoy playing consequences – it's the ideal game to play on a rainy afternoon when there's nothing else to do! Take some pieces of paper measuring about 6cm × 8cm. Give everyone a piece and also a pencil. Ask them all to write a breed of animal at the top of the paper – it could be anything, from an ant to a zebra – and then fold the top of the paper over so that the animal is hidden. Now pass the papers round two people to the left and, under the folded over part, write an every-day activity. Again this could be anything you like, from baking a cake to tying your shoelaces. Fold the papers over again and pass them round to the left.

Everyone should now open their sheet and read what they've got. Without telling anybody which animal or activity you've been given, you must take it in turns to stand up and give your impression. You can only sit down when they have guessed what you are and what you're doing.

This game can be hysterically funny. After all, have you ever tried imitating a pig playing the violin or a cat cooking an omelette before?

Famous Names Consequences

Like Animal Consequences, all the players have a sheet of paper and a pencil. Start by writing the name of a famous person, one whom everyone will recognise, at the top. Fold the paper over and pass it round. Now everyone writes down a location. For example, you could have 'Up a tree' or 'On a bus'. Again, fold the papers and pass them round. This time everyone writes down a common activity – like peeling potatoes or reading a newspaper. Fold over the papers, pass them round once more and then open them up. Everyone should take turns to act out the person, the location and the activity. You think it sounds easy? Okay, how would *you* do an impression of the Princess of Wales in a rowing boat doing the washing-up?

Pass the Orange

Divide all your guests into two teams and ask the members of each team to line up behind each other. Give the first player in each team an orange and get them to hold it under their chin. When you tell them to start they must turn round and, using *just* their chins and *not* their hands, the next person must take it from them and pass it on in turn. Everyone must stay in character while they're playing, of course. The first team to pass the orange to the last player wins the game. Just as funny is a similar game where the players pass the outer sleeve of a matchbox on their noses. Try it, it's almost impossible!

LET'S PUT ON A SHOW

The first time I appeared on stage things didn't go as well as I'd hoped. I walked out in front of the audience carrying my guitar and found that the microphone had been adjusted to its lowest position – about level with my waist! Instead of turning the little knob and raising it I bent right over and sang into the microphone. So for the first song I ever sang on stage, all the audience could see was the top of my head!

If, like me, you really love doing impressions, why not use your comedy skills to put on a show? If you've worked long and hard to perfect them you deserve the chance to perform in front of an audience. Who knows, you may turn out to be a star!

WHEN AND WHERE:
There are all kinds of opportunities for you to put on a show. You could start by entertaining your family and friends in your own home. I suppose that's how I started, by making my friends laugh. If you are more ambitious, get together with a few talented pals and put on a performance in the garden. You could invite everyone's family to come along and watch – you might even try asking them to pay for tickets!

On a more ambitious scale, many schools have a week each year when the pupils spend their time raising money for charity. If your school does this, why not ask your drama and music teachers if they can help you organise a variety show packed with impressions? You could call it the 'All-Star Revue' and charge your audience to come in and see the show.

I'm a Vice President of the National Association of Boys Clubs and I know that many organisations like Boys Clubs, and the Scouts and Guides, are *always* looking for ideas to raise money. If you're a member of one of these or a similar organisation, you could suggest to your leader that you put on a fund-raising evening of music and entertainment. Naturally, the larger the scale on which you're going to perform, the more hard work you'll have to put into the rehearsing and preparation of your show and the more performers and assistants you'll need. But whatever kind of show you want to put on, you'll need material to perform!

WRITING MATERIAL:
Probably the most important thing of all when it comes to entertaining your audience is the material you use – the jokes you tell and the sketches and songs you participate in. I realised this after my first few public performances. My act went down very well in one club in north London and I was asked if I would go back and

perform again the next week. When I turned up a week later I discovered that the audience consisted mainly of people who had been there the week before and had heard my jokes already! That taught me to keep developing new material and not to rely on old jokes too much. Here's some more advice I'd like to pass on to you.

Try to fill your show with lots of brief scenes and jokes. This is safer than trying to do a long and complicated play which might go wrong and which the audience might not like very much! If every sketch and scene you do only lasts a couple of minutes no one will have time to get bored. Anyway, short sketches are much funnier than long plays!

Before you start to write your material spend a few days watching all the television comedy programmes you can. Notice how they include a mixture of scenes and sketches and how many of them are full of old jokes and slapstick routines. If you think any of them are really funny, make a note of them and adapt them for use in your own show. Of course you mustn't copy the TV sketch – lots of the people in the audience might have seen it too and they will know that it's not original!

When it comes to actually writing the material, gather together everyone who is going to be in your show and work out which impressions they do best and which parts they are willing to play. Get them to throw in all their ideas. Then start writing seriously.

Here is a rough idea of how you might organise some of the scenes using the characters mentioned in this book:

1 *The introduction.* For this you might perform a funny song featuring everyone in the show. How about taking a famous song and changing the words to make it appropriate to the occasion?

2 *A stand-up comedy act.* Ask one of the performers who imitates a comedian to do a stand-up routine with lots of jokes and stories. You'll find plenty of the basic material in the **JOKE FILE** chapter. Choose jokes that suit the character and string them together with some linking ideas.

3 *A sketch.* Try a 'Doctor, Doctor' sketch with several characters coming on, one after another, to tell the doctor their problem. For the doctor use a funny character – Jimmy Cricket perhaps. All the characters should have a suitable problem. Alexis from *Dynasty* could walk on in a mink coat and say, 'Doctor, doctor, I'm boiling,' to which the doctor replies, 'Simmer down, now. Simmer down.' Peggy from *Hi De Hi* could come in and say, 'It's awful, Doctor! I feel like a soft drink!' to which the doctor's answer is, 'I warned you not to play squash.' And so on!

4 *An awful magician.* How about having Jimmy Krankie doing magic tricks – and getting them all wrong! For this sketch you could ask someone to come out from the audience to give you a hand and make them do all sorts of silly things.

5 *A sketch with just a couple of characters.* Did you see the tremendously funny scene on television in which Frank Bruno and Lenny Henry played Romeo and Juliet? Try something similar but with different characters. How about having Hilda Ogden from *Coronation Street* playing Juliet and Darth Vader as Romeo?

6 *A song or dance act.* Now is the time for someone to perform their impression of a pop singer. Try Barry Manilow or Ben Volpeliere-Pierrot. Rather than just copying them, do something silly – like having Barry's nose fall off or Ben's legs get tangled up!

7 *Another sketch with several people.* Perhaps this time you could do a version of *Grange Hill*? Call it Strange Hill and have all your characters behaving in the way they used to when they were at school. Sir Robin Day could take the role of the teacher! Adrian Mole and Jimmy Krankie could be schoolboys and you could also include Madonna and Angie from *EastEnders* as naughty schoolgirls. Again, you will find some suitable jokes in the **JOKE FILE** chapter. You can add new material of your own too!

8 *A 'speciality' act performed by one of the characters.* Perhaps you could make it a crazy cookery spot in which one of the characters makes some horrible recipe – and a lot of mess! (If you're

going to make a mess in any way, put down a large sheet of plastic and make sure that you don't damage anything!)

9 *A final sketch.* One of the secrets of writing sketches is to transform a situation by putting it into a new place. For example, how about setting the scene in the bar of the Queen Vic from *EastEnders* but transforming it into the year 2010? There are all kinds of jokes you could play here. Try dressing up in futuristic costume or transforming Ethel the cleaning lady into Ethel the cleaning robot who runs wild!

10 *The finale.* Another song featuring everyone in the show. Try rewriting Frank Sinatra's great hit 'My Way' and making it 'Our Way', for example.

GARY'S STAR TIP

If you're worried that the audience won't be able to keep up with what's going on in your show, you could use one of the characters as a compere to introduce each act and sketch in turn. That reminds me of the time I ended up being a compere at a charity performance of a pantomime. For this one special night, the panto had been rewritten so that everyone swapped parts! They decided to have a pantomime horse as the compere and Andrea Arnold, who you may have seen on *No 73*, was the front half. She was doing it very well, coming to the front of the stage and saying her lines, until she came on to introduce the fifth or sixth scene and walked straight off the edge of the stage and fell into the orchestra pit! There was a long silence and one or two people jumped into the orchestra pit to see if she was all right. She was, fortunately, but she was badly shaken and couldn't continue. It looked as if they were going to be without a compere for the rest of the evening so I dashed behind the scenes and offered to be the front half of the horse. They said it was all right, so I scribbled down a few silly rhymes about Andrea's accident and climbed into the costume. To make it look even funnier than it was, as I walked across the stage I kept feeling out with one foot to make sure that we weren't in any danger of falling off the edge!

****

GARY'S STAR TIP

Keep your show moving as fast as possible! *Don't* waste time climbing in and out of costumes and shifting scenery because that allows the audience to get bored. None of my impressions take more than a few seconds to prepare, and that's something I'm very careful about. Some of my costumes are specially designed so that I can change into them quickly and I don't bother with a lot of wigs and make-up. *Remember:* no one will believe that you are really Madonna or Stevie Wonder no matter how long you spend preparing yourself. In fact it may be funnier if you don't look anything like them at all!

****

REMEMBER: Putting on a show is very hard work and you will need to spend days and days writing, rehearsing and getting things organised. But it's worth it if you want to make The Right Impression!

ROLF HARRIS

YOUR CARTOON TIME

Did you know that you can draw?

Rolf Harris shows you how – clearly and simply – in YOUR CARTOON TIME. Starting with stick figures, he explains how to develop these step-by-step into your own stylish characters, and there are ideas too for how you can use your drawings – as birthday cards, home movies and so on.

Drawing is fun!

All you need is pencil, paper and Rolf Harris's book – YOUR CARTOON TIME!

KNIGHT BOOKS

ROLF HARRIS

A CATALOGUE OF COMIC VERSE

A cattledog (as they say in Australia!) jam-packed with great poems on a variety of different topics – including cats and dogs – and to say nothing of tigers and terrified tortoises, some rather curious eating habits and some loony relations.

This rumbustious collection for children of all ages has been compiled and interpreted with refreshing drawings by Rolf Harris.

KNIGHT BOOKS

WELCOME TO THE WORLD OF MASK –
Mobile Armoured Strike Kommand where
illusion and deception team up with man and
machine.

BOOK 1: THE DEATHSTONE
The MASK mission: to recover the meteor –
The Deathstone – with the assistance of
Matt Trakker, his son Scott and his loyal com-
panion T-Bob.

MASK – where illusion is the ultimate
weapon!

KNIGHT BOOKS

THE REAL GHOSTBUSTERS™

BOOK 1: JANINE'S GENIE

Ghostbusters are here to save the world!

The Real Ghostbusters have arrived, and they're the hottest, spook-hunting brains on the streets. Four brave men, one daring woman, and Slimer, one crazy lump of green ectoplasm set on a mission of high-class ghost-trapping – where no spirit has a ghost of a chance!

When a client offers the Ghostbusters the pick of his belongings instead of payment, Janine chooses a ridiculous, old brass oil-lamp and unleashes a load of trouble on to town in the shape of a lampful of ghosts and ghouls.

KNIGHT BOOKS

CAROL VORDERMAN

DIRTY, LOUD AND BRILLIANT

Bet you can't
* hold a cup with one finger
* light a torch with a lemon
* make a table top hovercraft

With DIRTY, LOUD AND BRILLIANT – you can! Masses of easy-to-follow mind-boggling experiments using stuff you'll find at home. Fantastic experiments by television's science wizz.

Have a Dirty, Loud and Brilliant time!

KNIGHT BOOKS

Post·A·Book